ROUTLEDGE LIBRARY EDITIONS: LIBRARY AND INFORMATION SCIENCE

Volume 97

TRAINING ISSUES AND STRATEGIES IN LIBRARIES

TRAINING ISSUES AND STRATEGIES IN LIBRARIES

Edited by
PAUL M. GHERMAN AND
FRANCES O. PAINTER

LONDON AND NEW YORK

First published in 1990 by The Haworth Press, Inc.

This edition first published in 2020
by Routledge
2 Park Square, Milton Park, Abingdon, Oxon OX14 4RN

and by Routledge
52 Vanderbilt Avenue, New York, NY 10017

Routledge is an imprint of the Taylor & Francis Group, an informa business

© 1990 The Haworth Press, Inc.

All rights reserved. No part of this book may be reprinted or reproduced or utilised in any form or by any electronic, mechanical, or other means, now known or hereafter invented, including photocopying and recording, or in any information storage or retrieval system, without permission in writing from the publishers.

Trademark notice: Product or corporate names may be trademarks or registered trademarks, and are used only for identification and explanation without intent to infringe.

British Library Cataloguing in Publication Data
A catalogue record for this book is available from the British Library

ISBN: 978-0-367-34616-4 (Set)
ISBN: 978-0-429-34352-0 (Set) (ebk)
ISBN: 978-0-367-42022-2 (Volume 97) (hbk)
ISBN: 978-0-367-82156-2 (Volume 97) (ebk)

Publisher's Note
The publisher has gone to great lengths to ensure the quality of this reprint but points out that some imperfections in the original copies may be apparent.

Disclaimer
The publisher has made every effort to trace copyright holders and would welcome correspondence from those they have been unable to trace.

Training Issues and Strategies in Libraries

Paul M. Gherman
Frances O. Painter
Editors

The Haworth Press
New York • London

Training Issues and Strategies in Libraries has also been published as *Journal of Library Administration*, Volume 12, Number 2 1990.

© 1990 by The Haworth Press, Inc. All rights reserved. No part of this work may be reproduced or utilized in any form or by any means, electronic or mechanical, including photocopying, microfilm and recording, or by any information storage and retrieval system, without permission in writing from the publisher. Printed in the United States of America.

The Haworth Press, Inc., 10 Alice Street, Binghamton, NY 13904-1580
EUROSPAN/Haworth, 3 Henrietta Street, London WC2E 8LU England

Library of Congress Cataloging-in-Publication Data

Training issues and strategies in libraries / Paul M. Gherman, Frances O. Painter, editors.
    p. cm.
  "Has also been published as Journal of library administration, volume 12, number 2, 1990" – T.p. verso.
  Includes bibliographical references.
  ISBN 0-86656-937-5
  1. Library education. 2. Library employees – Training of. I. Gherman, Paul M. II. Painter, Frances O.
Z668.T73   1990
023'.8 – dc20   90-4221
                                                                                          CIP

Training Issues and Strategies in Libraries

CONTENTS

Introduction
    Paul M. Gherman
    Frances O. Painter
	1

Vendor Training: A Question of Commitment to User Success *Charles A. Litchfield*	3

Front-End Analysis: Aligning Library Planning, Resources, and Commitment to ILS Staff Training
    Stuart J. Glogoff
    James P. Flynn
	13

Training for Public Services
    Elena E. Cevallos
    Charles E. Kratz
	27

Options in Learning: Instructor Led and Computer Based Training (CBT) *Janet L. Mushrush*	47
Preparing for Library Leadership *Susan Jurow*	57
Training Endusers/Remote Users *Joe Jaros*	75
Student Staff Training in the Smaller Library *Ruth Ann Edwards*	89

Introduction

Each new wave of technology washes over us and in doing so makes obsolete many of our skills. Training, whether we like it or not, must be on everyone's agenda; both their personal as well as their library agenda. Training can no longer be an add-on after all else is taken care of, but it must be an integral part of each manager's strategic plan.

In *Thriving on Chaos*, Tom Peters lists training as one of the key areas to be emphasized if an organization is to survive in our changing world. He states, "The innovation prescriptions were clear—everyone must innovate. Everyone *must* be prepared (1) to contribute to ideas and (2) to work together with less supervision. And only constant training will provide the basis for constant adaptation."[1] In libraries today, change is the very essence of our lives, and each change amplifies those before at an ever increasing pace. Fear, burn-out, and the obsolescence of our skills plague library personnel, as we wonder if our very institutions will survive.

It began slowly with the automation of a few library activities on mainframes, then came local turn-key systems, then the networks as our technical services shifted to a national plane, then the PC and word processing, spreadsheets, and a host of specialized software, then online databases, then CD ROM and a new realm of storage, and now the prospect of locally mounted mainframe databases, telecommunications, and the possibility of a national internet linking many types of end-users. Just the release of OCLC's New System will mean countless hours of training for participating libraries. And the strategic decision such as whether the library community should cling to OSI versus the TCIP/IP model for telecommunications, is but one of the highly technical decisions we must make based on a new knowledge base which few librarians have.

More of our training is being transferred to metalibrary organizations such as OCLC or RLG and state and regional networks. Ven-

© 1990 by The Haworth Press, Inc. All rights reserved.

dors also play an increasing role in training, as well as our professional societies, such as ALA and ARL. A forward thinking library takes responsibility for the training and development of its personnel. A vital training program provides, updates, and enhances the skills that make library staff successful in the current workplace. In today's bottom line conscious environment, training can make an obvious contribution by reducing turnover, and by identifying high performers for key jobs. Today's rapidly changing information technology mandates an organized training program, lest our staff members muddle through, getting by but not getting the best from the new resource, because no one has taken the time to train.

This special collection on training has several articles by individuals working in metalibrary organizations providing training. Other authors give us perspectives on training from a small college library to a larger research library's strategies for effectively using the latest technology. Another explores our responsibility to our profession to recognize and develop leaders from within. This collection provides ideas and direction for ensuring that our staffs are able to keep up with changes in the resources available in our libraries and to keep ahead of changes in the expectations of our clientele.

We all know that change costs money. However, deferring staff training is economy dearly bought. Human resource practitioners tell us that in the workplace of the 1990's, employee selection will be much less effective in ensuring the knowledge, skills, and abilities we need in our organizations—employee training will be the key. To be flexible and responsive to changes in the fast moving information technology environment, training is an essential.

Paul M. Gherman
Frances O. Painter

NOTE

1. Tom Peters, *Thriving on Chaos: Handbook for a Management Revolution.* (New York: Alfred A. Knopf, 1987), p. 324.

Vendor Training: A Question of Commitment to User Success

Charles A. Litchfield

SUMMARY. The article explores the role of vendor training in the long-term relationship that exists between libraries that purchase an integrated online library system and vendors that market and support such systems. Emphasis is given to the responsibility vendors have to properly train library personnel so as to insure successful implementation and use of their online system. Analysis and evaluation of vendor training programs is stressed and suggestions are given for how vendors can possibly improve the training provided to their users.

When buying a commercially developed integrated on-line library system (IOLS), a library must recognize the long term dependent relationship that is established with the vendor of that system (1). Until the library abandons the system for another or the vendor ceases to support the system, the library is locked into a symbiotic relationship that can effect its operations for many years. The process where by both parties commit to this relationship usually involves a mating ritual of epic proportion. An aspect of the procurement procedure that deserves more attention is the analysis of training opportunities offered by the system vendor. To a large extent, the vendor's commitment to proper training will mirror its

---

Charles A. Litchfield is Retrospective Conversion Coordinator at Newman Library, Virginia Polytechnic Institute and State University, in Blacksburg, VA.

© 1990 by The Haworth Press, Inc. All rights reserved.

commitment to the library's successful implementation and maintenance of the system over the length of the vendor/library relationship.

All too often the aspect of vendor training is taken too lightly in the analysis and purchase of integrated online systems. Given the wide range of topics that must be covered when reviewing different systems, writing RFP's, and negotiated contracts, etc., it is understandable that training can slip to a secondary status. This unfortunate circumstance can prove to be very costly in the long run, if ignored until after a contract is signed. To accept the idea that training is basically an "in-house" process, and therefore of lesser importance during initial purchase agreements, negates the vendor's long term responsibility for the successful use of the system. Training users of integrated online library systems, staff as well as patrons, must be viewed as an ongoing process (2). It should be seen as a cooperative venture between the library and the system vendor. Success in this area should be sought when analyzing different systems, documented in great detail on RFP's and purchase contracts, and demanded from vendors as long as their system is in use.

TRAINING FROM THE VENDOR'S PERSPECTIVE

It is understood that, to remain viable, commercial vendors of IOLS's must make a profit (3). In order to stay in business they must sustain their operations, support future development activity and show a return on investment. Basically, they attempt to charge as much as possible for the best system they can develop for the least amount of money. To a large extent corporate emphasis is placed on sales, to generate revenue, and development, to generate future sales. Training and maintenance, for those who have "signed on the dotted line," often take a back seat to the quest for new customers and system enhancements that will attract new sales. Even when a vendor reaches a point where annual maintenance fees become a significant portion of annual revenues, existing customers are viewed as a captive audience, with little or no influence when compared to the next potential sale.

The impact of this type of corporate philosophy on user training can be tremendous. No matter what is stated either before or after a contract is signed, the vendor will usually attempt to provide only a minimal level of training. The cost of sending company professionals on the road to provide onsight training involves very expensive manhours that eat heavily into the quarterly profit margin. Also, the same individuals are usually part of the maintenance team back at the home office, so their absence can cause a drop in maintenance service to the rest of the user community. The vendor, therefore, has a vested interest in limiting the amount of training to the lowest level acceptable to a customer. Most vendors use a combination of two philosophies to accomplish this goal: they stress the "user friendly" nature of their system and they attempt to only "train the trainers," who then become responsible for training the rest of the library's staff and patrons.

In the first instance, by stressing how user friendly a system is, a vendor can down play the need for extensive training. A run down of the commands necessary for operating each module is thought to be adequate, combined with help screens and an armful of user's manuals. Systems personnel, on the average, receive the most training because very few libraries will release funds to a vendor if the system is not up and running. The effective use of the system once the lights begin to blink and records begin to load can be a totally different story. If a library, on its own, cannot successfully implement a "user friendly" system that has been installed in other libraries then the vendor can argue that the fault lies with the library, not the system.

The "train the trainers" method, as described by Matthews, Boss, and others, is often cited as the most successful way to implement a system training program (4). The idea centers on the notion that a vendor is only responsible for training a small core of library staff, who will then be responsible for training the rest of the staff and all patrons of the system. In-house training programs, while necessary because of staff turn over and the expense of follow up vendor training, should not abrogate the responsibility of the vendor to provide training of a sufficient detail to guarantee successful implementation of all aspects of a library's online system. By relying heavily on the "train the trainers" technique, the vendor can again cut down on the amount of training provided to a library and shift blame to the in-house training group should any difficulties arise after initial installation.

VENDOR TRAINING FROM THE LIBRARY'S PERSPECTIVE

In many instances, initial vendor training is an overwhelming and perplexing experience for library staff. For the first time, many employees are confronted by the inevitability of profound and all encompassing change. It is not unusual for staff to be resistant to the changes brought about by a new online system (5). New ways of performing old familiar tasks are presented. Long lists of computer commands and screen displays must be mastered. Local policies and procedures that may not apply in an online environment must be re-evaluated. Often, during vendor training, staff will realize that the system does not do what they thought it would do (or were led to believe it would do) in a given module. It is also possible that entire job classifications cease to exist (typists, filers, etc.) and new responsibilities are discussed (data entry operator, on-line data maintenance, etc.).

The upshot of this process can be that very little of initial vendor training sinks in and stays with the employees who are trained. The library ends up with a staff that is dazed and confused, and considers itself lucky if the user manuals are readable and the system commands all function as described. Once again, vendors rely on this phenomenon to get their trainers in and out of the library in the shortest time possible, leaving the library to bring up the systems' various capabilities in what ever combination of fits and starts they can muster. The initial training of staff is too important to the overall success of a new system to be dealt with in a cavalier manner. The success or failure of the automation system could depend on the attitude developed by the employees early in the implementation of the system. It is through the training process that library personnel overcome their resistance to change and forge a commitment to the new technology (6). Vendor training must occupy a larger role in this process.

CHANGING THE WAY VENDORS PROVIDE TRAINING

To begin with, libraries should adopt a higher level of expectations regarding vendor training. The more vague and ambiguous a vendor is about the training they provide the more cautious a library should be. When analyzing different systems or conducting onsight visits of current users, more detailed questions should be asked about the training provided by the vendors. Potential buyers should be concerned about how many trainers were sent by the vendor and how many staff members were trained. The number of days spent on each module should be assessed. Was their system operational at the time of training or were they trained on a test data base? Were manuals and users guides provided at the time of training, and if so, were they helpful and instructive? Did the trainers lecture, use overheads, and/or provide ample time for hands-on terminal interaction? Were the sessions rigid and highly structured or casual, free flowing and self-directed? Did production use of the system occur before, after or long after training was provided? To what effect? Were all modules of the system brought up together or phased in over time, and how did this affect the library's training program. These and many other training questions should be answered in the process of comparing different online systems.

When writing an RFP, which becomes part of the legal documentation of purchasing a system, be explicit in the section on vendor training. State in great detail what is expected from the vendor and make sure their quoted price includes what you expect to receive. Do not be bought off with boilerplate answers, such as "adequate training will be provided." Plan out your training needs and state them for each part of the system:

- 6 employees to be trained in systems operations for three days.
- 8 employees to be trained in circulation operations for two days.
- 10 employees to be trained in cataloging/data entry for two days.
- 6 employees to be trained in acquisitions/serials receiving for two days.

Or use open ended statements such as "up to six employees to be designated by the library, are to be trained . . ." Also, state specifiically every aspect to be covered in the training of each group. The vendor should be willing to ensure acceptable levels of operational proficiency in the staff to be trained (7).

When negotiating a final contract with a vendor be specific about how and when training will occur. Nail down the details of whether training occurs in-house or at their headquarters, on live data or a test database, what kind of special equipment is necessary and in what types of configurations. If the system is not coming up all at once, but spaced out over time, make sure that the training is similarly arranged. If certain modules or capabilities are under development and promised at some point in the future, make sure that future training obligations are explicitly stated and agreed upon (8). No new module, regardless of its capabilities, will be used to its full potential if it's poorly documented and the library staff receives little or no training. If possible, each major known enhancement should have a stated quantity of training associated with its arrival in the system. The implementation of modules such as acquisitions, serials control, key word searching, or authority control should include vendor training regardless of when the system is installed. A new user should make every attempt to have future training needs included in the initial purchase price.

A final aspect of vendor training that should be important to a library analyzing online library systems is the attitude of the vendor towards training in general. An attempt should be made to gauge the level of commitment a vendor demonstrates regarding training of staff and patrons in the libraries that purchase their systems. While subjective in nature, this analysis can be quantified to a certain extent.

To begin with, the vendor should provide information regarding how many employees they have that provide training, what their backgrounds are and the areas of training for which they are responsible. If the vendor has librarians with reference experience in small public libraries doing technical services training in large academic libraries then the vendor's priorities need to be questioned. Also, the vendor should divulge what percentage of the support staff is devoted to training and what other duties they may perform. This gives a good indication of the level of importance placed on training by the vendor, and reveals what type of relationship exists between training staff and user support staff.

The vendors should make available examples of user manuals, training workbooks, searching guides, etc., that are provided when a system is purchased and users are trained. There should be evidence that the material is kept up to date as the system changes. Agreements as to how many copies of each are to be provided and maintained should be explicitly stated in RFP's and purchase contracts. Training materials should then be evaluated like any other aspect of the system. Is the text easy to understand, are there enough examples, do the examples properly illustrate the processes being described? Is the material meant only for initial training of staff or is some of it designed for future in-house training of staff and patrons? Is the material rigid, inflexible, generic in nature, or can it be altered to satisfy particular training needs in your library? Again, a library should review this material in an effort to gauge the vendor's commitment to a user's successful implementation of the system.

Vendors should also have available complete refresher courses for every aspect of their system. Regardless of the quality of initial training and system documentation, it may be necessary at some time in the future for various library staff members to be retrained. Just as system hardware and software change and evolve, so do library managers and support staff. Vendors should provide a full array of training opportunities that allow new staff or staff with new responsibilities to be brought up to speed on the system as quickly as possible. These courses should be reasonably priced and available both in-house and at vendor designated locations on a regularly scheduled basis. Ongoing training courses demonstrate the vendor's commitment to continued training of existing users and provide libraries with the opportunity to remain current with their system's capabilities.

Possible Training Innovations

An area of vendor training needing substantial improvement is the assistance they provide to in-house training programs. Whether highly structured or informal, libraries are continuously instructing patrons and staff in the use of their integrated online system. Turn over in new patrons and staff require ongoing basic training, while enhancements to the system require retraining of patrons and staff already familiar with the system. Vendors should play a more active role in the in-house training process.

It is essential that vendors go beyond these initial training obligations and take more seriously, their responsibility to "train the trainers." More adequate training tools should be developed and made available to libraries attempting to establish in-house training programs. Teaching manuals, different from operating manuals, should exist for every major function of a system. Workbooks, allowing self-directed instruction, could easily be provided, and made flexible to the point that each library could tailor them to suit their particular needs. With the rapid advances in desktop publishing it would be simple for vendors to provide basic training documents that could be locally adapted and printed out as needed. The necessary software could be provided with the initial purchase, or sold separately, and maintained through annual fees.

Other training tools currently ignored by most vendors of integrated library systems include videotape, instructional television and computer assisted instruction (CAI). Individual libraries find it difficult to develop these training devices on their own because of high cost and lack of expertise (9). Vendors, however, could more easily develop the necessary capabilities and recoup their production costs through sales to users of their system.

Another training tool of great importance is the locally controlled training/test database. Vendors would be well advised to support and encourage the use of test databases in conjunction with main library systems. The training uses for test databases can be tremendous (10). During initial implementation of the system library staff can be trained on a separate test database without waiting for or interfering with the creation of the "real" database. After implementation of the system a test database can be used to create in-house programs for bibliographic instruction of patrons, or training sessions for new staff. When new features are added to the system they can be implemented first in a test database, allowing staff to be trained without fear of compromising "real" data. A test database also allows system personnel an opportunity to experiment with new or different database management functions without disrupting the operation of the library's online system.

The use of a test database can be invaluable when testing a new version of vendor software. If the conversion programs include design changes in the structure of existing datasets, it can prove to be quite difficult and time consuming to return to the previous version of software should anything go wrong in the conversion process. By converting the test database first the library systems personnel can test the procedures involved before committing the entire library system to the conversion process. Many hours of downtime and loss of system access can thus be avoided.

These types of improvements to systems training should be a continual goal of every library automation vendor. The fact that most libraries are forced to "reinvent the wheel" when it comes to training for use of an automated system will become less and less acceptable. Successful training packages should be an integral part of every integrated library system.

CONCLUSION

Not long ago, an editorial in Library Journal used the phrase "enlightened self-interest" to describe certain vendor activities that reduce hostilities and build trust in the library field. Through various donations of time, money, and material vendors have improved the practice of librarianship while at the same time creating profit opportunities for themselves (11). A similar attitude needs to pervade the area of vendor training.

In the next five to ten years, if estimates prove correct, the majority of libraries in this country, other than school libraries, will be automated in some form (12). As the market for integrated library systems shrinks it is quite possible that the number and variety of commercially vended library systems will begin to dwindle. Should this happen, the systems that survive are going to need a broad base of successful satisfied users. As libraries seek to upgrade their outdated systems or are forced to seek new systems because of vendor demise, successful implementation and user satisfaction will take on greater and greater importance. It would be a definite sign of "enlightened self-interest" for vendors to take a long, hard look at their training programs. Their future success may depend on how successfully they train their current users.

REFERENCES

1. Richard De Gennaro, "Integrated Online Library Systems: Perspectives, Perceptions, and Practicalities," Library Journal 110:2 (February 1985), p.39.

2. Ellen Hoffmann, "Managing Automation: A Process, Not a Project," Library HiTech 6:1 (1988), p.50-51; Stuart Glogoff and James P. Flynn, "Developing a Systematic In-house Training Program for Integrated Library Systems," College and Research Libraries 48 (November 1987), p.528.

3. Richard De Gennaro, "Doing business with Vendors in the Computer-Based Library Systems Marketplace," American Libraries, 9 (April 1978), p.222; Victor Rosenberg, "A Partnership To Build: Librarians and Software Producers," Wilson Library Bulletin 62 (October 1987), p.33.

4. Richard W. Boss, The Library Manager's Guide to Automation, 2d.ed. (White Plains, N.Y.: Knowledge Industry, c.1984), p.112; Joseph R. Matthews, ed., A Reader on Choosing an Automated Library System (Chicago: American Library Association, 1983), p.201.

5. Michael Malinconico, "Hearing the Resistance," Library Journal 108:2 (January 15, 1983), p.111-113; "Listening to the Resistance," Library Journal 108:4 (February 15, 1983), p.353-355.

6. Sara F. Fine, "Technological Innovation, Diffusion and Resistance: An Historical Perspective," Journal of Library Administration 7:1 (Spring 1986), p.100.

7. Dennis Reynolds, Library Automation: Issues and Applications (New York: R. Bowker Co., 1985), p. 260.

8. Ibid., p.260.

9. Noelle Van Pudis, "User Education for an Online Catalog: A Workshop Approach," RQ 21 (Fall 1981), p.64; Rowena W. Swanson, "An Assessment of Online Instruction Methodologies," Online 6 (January 1982), p.45.

10. Barbara G. Smith and Marily Borgendale, "The Second Time Around: The Next Generation Local Online System," Library Journal 113:12 (July 1988), p.51.

11. John Barry, "The Enlightened Vendor," Library Journal 113:12 (July 1988), p.4.

12. Richard W. Boss, "Technology and the Modern Library," Library Journal 109:11 (June 15, 1984), p. 1189.

Front-End Analysis: Aligning Library Planning, Resources, and Commitment to ILS Staff Training

Stuart J. Glogoff
James P. Flynn

SUMMARY. When a library is implementing an integrated library system, the library administrator needs a staff training program that applies management concepts to the overall strategic plan. The authors recommend a modified form of Joseph Harless' Front-End Analysis problem solving model which is designed to force the user to think through the underlying conditions or terms creating the "problem" environment and then link solutions to a training model. A 2 phase approach is presented that is structured around defining the problem state and delineating the specific steps to correct problem areas. A time analysis of the authors' initial staff training program is outlined and 2 sample needs assessments are provided.

During a discussion on preparing a staff training session for our integrated library system (ILS), a colleague remarked that the Chinese curse "May you live in exciting times," seemed most appropriate. Certainly, implementing an ILS is exciting. With it, however, comes the curse of applying this new, expensive system in a manner that maximizes its potential benefits. Indeed, the obligation to meet successfully the short-term and long-term objectives of an ILS are great. Implementation touches the work of nearly all library employees and, like other programs, requires library administrators to detail a clearly defined plan. Central to this implementation plan

---

Stuart J. Glogoff is Librarian and Head of the Systems Department at the University of Delaware Library, in Newark, DE.
James P. Flynn is Director of Personnel Services at the University of Delaware, in Newark, DE.

© 1990 by The Haworth Press, Inc. All rights reserved.

is a staff training program that takes into account the considerable human and material resources required. This article exposes a model of training based on the concept of Front-End Analysis that library administrators can use to effectively implement an ILS.

BACKGROUND

Recent data from William Saffady and Richard Boss show that there is a substantial market for integrated multi-function library systems. Saffady tallied an estimated 995 integrated systems either installed or contracted for in North American libraries through June 1987 [1] while Boss's statistics for operational systems throughout the world at the end of 1987 reached approximately 2,000 sites [2]. Boss also provides some illuminating numbers showing the volume of turnkey sales since the mid-1980's (1984: 232, 1985: 196, 1986: 210, 1987: 350) [3]. Saffady points out that over 34% of currently operating systems were installed more than 5 years ago and are, consequently, candidates for replacement and that by 1990, over 54% of currently installed systems will be more than 5 years old [4]. The trend is clearly that automated systems are a continuing fact of library administration.

Surely such a level of activity should result in a substantial number of reports on systematic implementation plans in the professional literature. Surprisingly, this is not the case. One may speculate that there are primarily 2 explanations. First, the procurement phase for an ILS is an extraordinary effort marked by uncertainty and linked to funding, local computing support, consortium politics and the sometimes precarious state of the marketplace. So much energy is expended acquiring a system that developing an action plan for implementation lags. Secondly, there is the role played by consultants and vendors. Consultants work with libraries during the procurement phase and their participation usually culminates in negotiating a contract. Advice on implementation may identify concerns such as site preparation, database conversion, training technical staff, system acceptance and library staff training but does not approach the level of involvement of the procurement phase. Vendors, on the other hand, are adept at providing technical specifications to install the system but tend to provide painfully little realistic information on the local resources needed to train staff and document the system. Saffady found in his survey that few libraries found the vendor provided training beneficial. In fact, "most considered it marginally acceptable, and some indicated that after the initial session, they did not bother to schedule their remaining training days." [5] Vendor training was typically supplemented by workshops conducted by library staff members and, overall, that staff training tended to be self-perpetuating, with some sites providing occasional workshops to meet staff needs. In addition, Saffady relayed the comments from many sites to plan to condense and rewrite the vendor's user manuals which were labeled as "poorly written, contained incomplete and confusing discussions of most system capabilities and omitted many topics." [6]

Of the attention given to ILS implementation in the professional literature or in presentations at conferences, most tends to be couched amid caveats or present a farraginous approach. These themes seem to be: beware that changes in internal operations can force organizational changes; beware that automation can impose a powerful psychological presence upon staff; here is what happened to our cataloging/acquisitions/serials/circulation department once automation was introduced.

The number of libraries acquiring an ILS over the past 5 years is a testimony to its value: improved use of the facility; increased operational effectiveness of staff; and better service to constituency groups. Nevertheless, a question remains regarding whether these libraries are receiving the best possible return on the time, staff, and funds invested in their ILS. In an earlier article [7], the authors presented the theoretical concepts behind the need to develop a systematic staff training program. This paper suggests that by incorporating a staff training program that applies management concepts to the library's overall strategic plan, a vision of how to create and administer implementation of an ILS and how to maintain it within a continuing organizational scheme becomes clear.

FRONT-END ANALYSIS (FEA)

Traditionally, administrators have asked certain questions when implementing an automated system module. Some questions might be: what is the cost? what is the time commitment required of staff to learn the new system? What is the staff's attitude now? What should their attitude be? What specific skills will be needed? What changes will there be in policy and personnel? Problematic with this approach is that it may encourage an administrator's "jumping" to a solution rather than applying a rational model which accurately defines the problem and confirms that it can be addressed through training.

From the authors' experience, a more rational problem solving/training model was defined by Joseph Harless over 20 years ago. He proposed a "Front-End Analysis" (FEA) method that forced the user to think through the underlying conditions or terms creating the "problem" environment and then link solutions to a training model [8]. Harless argued that people perform job tasks incorrectly for one of three reasons: (1) they do not know how to do them; (2) they are prevented from doing them correctly; or (3) they lack the incentive to do them [9]. These concerns must be acknowledged and compared against the overall management plan in order to achieve appropriate results. The authors have adopted a modified form of Harless' FEA problem solving model.

This problem solving model does not preclude using any of the standard "tools" (such as needs assessment instruments, direct observation, client feedback, or actual program monitoring) which library administrators may have found helpful. Focus groups can also be utilized to take advantage of the employee's expertise rather than repressing it. Recent literature such as *In Search of Excellence* stress the great creative power which can be unleashed when managers and their staffs are able to address problems directly — particularly when there is clear indication that their suggestions will be implemented.

The problem solving model proposed by the authors is presented in 2 phases. Phase I begins with the assumption that it is necessary to define the current situation (problem state) before one can develop the strategy and tactics to correct it. In fact, the extent of any problem is nothing more than the difference(s) between the current (unsatisfactory) conditions and a more desirable (satisfactory) state. The second phase concentrates on delineating the specific steps to correct these problem areas (see Table 1).

TABLE 1: THE FEA TRAINING MODEL

<u>Phase I: Problem Definition</u>

Current Situation	Contributing Factors	Causes
problem	1	1
	2	2
	3	3
	.	.
Desired	.	.
Situation	n	n

<u>Phase II: The Action Plan</u>

Corrective Steps	Timetable	Resource Requirement(s)
1		- Capital
2		- Human
3		- Facilities
.		- Equipment
.		
n		

For example, many library administrators view golf as a healthy and relaxing activity. They fantasize about the joy of walking the links with friends while executing long drives, graceful iron shots, and perfectly placed putts. For all their good feelings about the game, some library administrators are reluctant to play as frequently as they would like because of real or perceived performance deficiencies. Their game would be more beneficial if their performance level could improve. To improve their game though, our library linksters must first identify specific deficiencies.

How can this be done? One method is to consult outside sources: fellow players, the club pro, or any of the numerous pamphlets, videotapes, or books on the subject. Each of these resources offers a particular perspective on "effective" golf. Another method might be to videotape their drives, chip shots and putting styles. Viewing the tapes in the privacy of their homes, they can compare their actual performance on the golf course with the instructions garnered from the above resources.

These comparisons between desired performance (club pro, instructional materials) and actual performance (friends' observations, videotapes) form the basis of understanding the deficiencies being faced. Perhaps several elements contribute to their problems: poor foot stance, jerking the head, bad grip, and underweight clubs. For each of these contributing factors, our library administrators must determine *why* that factor is problematic and *how* to resolve it. For example, poor foot stance may explain why drives are hooking or slicing; jerking the head could be the cause of topping the ball on iron shots; not getting sufficient distance on shots might be attributable to underweight clubs; and a bad grip could explain why putts are consistently right of the cup. Each contributing factor has a causal basis. To resolve the undesirable situation those causes must be exposed and addressed.

When our library administrators have completed the first phase of golfing FEA, they will have:

1. Defined the differences between the current situation and the desired state;
2. Identified several major factors contributing to their problems; and
3. Analyzed why each factor is significant and determine how to correct it by performance improvement.

The next phase of the FEA involves an Action Plan to reduce/eliminate the contributing factors noted in point 2 above and move toward a solution. An Action Plan must be assembled in such a manner that successful implementation of any changes includes recognition of resource limitations such as practice time, physical stamina, money, or facilities. It is essential, however, that prior to beginning the action planning mode, a reasonable assessment of resource availability successfully be undertaken. In the authors' view, many well-intentioned training (performance improvement) efforts prove fruitless because a realistic assessment has not taken place. When the resource assessment activity has been concluded, the Action Plan can begin by developing specific tactics to address each of the contributing elements identified earlier.

Applying this to our golfing librarian example, our subject may conclude that foot placement is corrected by pointing the tip of the left shoe toward a spot on the back of the club. A bad grip may be corrected by aligning the fingers according to the Palmer Method before putting. Further, putting may be improved by spending 15 minutes on the putting green before each round. The matter of underweight clubs is obviously not a performance problem and can be corrected by matching the weight of the clubs to the golfer's height and weight. From the prior assessment, our subject knows the performance value of a suitable set of clubs and the cost for acquiring them. Another major element of FEA is Harless' strong contention that the value of performance improvement must exceed the costs associated with achieving it. If not, he argues, don't bother to influence the behavior. For a seminal analysis of cost/benefit issues in training, see the work of Gary A. Rummler [10].

With the tactics defined and the resources for needed improvement allocated, the Action Plan implementation phase can begin. At this point, adequate preparation needs to be made to assure that reasonable performance reviews are conducted and opportunities to improve/revise training strategies are included in the overall plan [11]. Having exposed a basic FEA through a not-too-serious example, we will now move to a discussion of applying FEA in a more "real-life" setting.

FRONT-END ANALYSIS IN ACTION

Prior to making any decisions to develop a staff training program at the authors' institution, it was recognized that the best method to assess staff strengths and deficiencies would be by distributing a needs assessment to all staff. A short cover acknowledged the valuable automated systems experience that many staff members already possessed. This experience, the memo stressed, offered a tremendous resource for developing an effective training program to support implementation. The needs assessment asked staff to help by identifying training techniques that worked for them. This approach gave staff the opportunity to exercise positive control in their new automated environment and potentially lessened possible resistance to the introduction of the new system [12]. By recognizing the human resource factors, grassroots support was invited and secured. This was proven through the active participation during the training cycle.

For the needs assessment instrument (see Appendix for Sample Needs Assessments), a general section solicited the degree of interest for workshops on such topics as: library automation terminology, computing terminology, various campus computing services, and other topics that staff suggested. Widespread interest in attending a series of such workshops was expressed. The primary section addressed training and sought to identify how staff had been trained on automated systems in the past. Questions were worded to encourage participation. For example, staff were asked what in their previous training experience did they consider "the single best training technique and would recommend be used" in our local program. Similarly, they were asked "what would you urge be avoided?" The responses to the needs assessment were reported in the library's in-house newsletter.

The needs assessment revealed that staff overwhelmingly preferred small group training with much hands-on experience. In addition, it was revealed that nearly all had been trained by a supervisor, co-worker, or gained skills osmotically while on-the-job. This lead to the conclusion that good and bad techniques may be practiced and reinforced with each generation of employee. Appropriately, the needs assessment had identified strengths and deficiencies. It was understood that a small group of trainers would be selected from among staff in all departments to develop an in-house training program for the online catalog and cataloging. A plan of action to realize this raised several questions. How can these persons best be prepared for the task? What library resources will be required? Are there external resources available to support the project? What is the proposed timetable?

The first step taken was to organize the trainers into a "focus group" and enlist the aid of a training specialist from the University's personnel office. The training specialist lead the focus groups through a series of workshops exploring adult learning theory, competency measurement, listening and questioning skills, developing training objectives and program design. Through the focus group approach, the trainers framed their past learning experiences on automated systems around sound staff training techniques. A basic level of knowledge was acquired in a positive environment while promoting enthusiasm for the project.

As the focus groups met to hone their training skills and develop a staff training program, administrative support was garnered by drafting a training statement that enlisted the support of administrative staff from department heads (middle managers) up to the director. This statement centralized administrative control for staff training on the new system and established the successful execution of the training program as a library goal [13]. It eliminated potential roadblocks by having each department head agree (1) to support the time trainers were required to spend in the focus groups and (2) to commit additional staff time for training and individual practice. The training statement was an important step to ensure that library staff would not find themselves in the confusing position of serving two masters.

Front-End analysis keeps the training officer ever mindful that the in-house staff training program must be flexible and offer numerous approaches to correct observed or possible performance deficiencies. When one approach does not work as well as expected, an alternative is identified. For example, introductory training for staff on the system's technical service module was based on the behavior modeling approach advocated by Kay Tytler Abella. This approach recommends giving training step-by-step instructions, demonstrations, discussions on technique, trial exercises, and feedback [14]. Unfortunately, this method proved extremely time consuming and repetitious for the trainers. As an alternative, a self-paced workbook with an online training file was prepared for staff. While one-on one training is still available if requested, the workbook has been an enormous boon to system trainers who can now apply their skills to advanced training for a select group. In addition, a more general approach has been developed to provide staff training or information on a variety of system related topics. A series of 20-30 minute presentations have been prepared (usually as "brown bag lunches") to provide general information. Topics include system hardware, software, and telecommunications; the MARC record and its relation to the local system; the local system's architecture and file structure; the workings of specific modules, like circulation and system security. Several of these topics were listed on the original needs assessment and other topics can be developed.

TIME ANALYSIS

As an example of the commitment a library administrator can expect to make to in-house staff training on an automated system, a time analysis of the authors' initial efforts is outlined. This first program was to train all library staff on the new system's online catalog. With hindsight, some aspects might have been conducted differently. Nevertheless, the organizational structure of this training program has withstood the test of time and three years later serves as the model for subsequent training projects. The steps listed below detail the elements of this initial program and approximate the total number of hours contributed by each participant category. For convenience, the following codes are used: CS = Campus specialist; STO = Systems training officer; L = Librarians; S = Support staff.

1. Pre-planning: system training officer and campus specialist review responses to the needs assessment and draft a plan of action which includes steps, timetable and resource requirements. CS: 10 hours; STO: 5 hours
2. System training officer presents training concept to other library administrators by outlining focus group concept, training plan, time commitment, and administrative commitment. STO: 1.5 hours
3. Trainers are appointed and their role is explained to them. A total of 11 staff members, including 4 librarians and 7 senior support staff will work with systems training officer. 4L: 1 hour; 7S: 1.75 hours
4. Systems training officer and campus specialist plan Workshop I for focus groups. Involves selecting reading material, discussion topics, scheduling, preparing materials for distribution. CS: 10 hours; STO: 5 hours

5. Workshop I: A 1.5 hour workshop discusses the difference between teaching and training, training techniques and approaches, and adult learning theory. CS: 2 hours; STO: 2 hours; 4L: 6 hours; 7S: 10.5 hours
6. Systems training officer and campus specialist prepare for Workshop II; trainers read and prepare to discuss 2 articles. CS: 5 hours; STO: 4 hours; 4L: 8 hours; 7S: 14 hours
7. Trainers attend vendor training session on online catalog and begin practicing on test database. STO: 10 hours; 4L: 24 hours; 7S: 42 hours
8. Workshop II: topics include skills acquisition, questioning techniques, answering techniques, one-on-one training and designing training sessions. Focus groups break down into smaller groups to develop a syllabus, user aids, exercises, scheduling procedures and promotional materials. CS: 2 hours; STO: 1.5 hours; 4L: 6 hours; 7S: 10.5 hours
9. Materials from small groups are drafted for other focus group members to review. 4L: 20 hours; 7S: 35 hours
10. Focus group meets to review, revise, and formalize syllabus, user aids and exercises. Training sessions dates are reserved, announced to all staff, and scheduled. STO: 4 hours; 4L: 8 hours; 7S: 25.5 hours
11. Trainers rehearse. 4L: 4 hours; 7S: 7 hours
12. Training begins: 1-2 trainers per session; 8 one hour slots per week over 4 weeks. STO: 4.5 hours; 4L: 15 hours; 7S: 25.5 hours
13. System training officer prepares and distributes evaluation questionnaire which is sent to all library staff. STO: 3 hours
14. Trainers review returned questionnaire and discuss possible training enhancements based on responses. STO: 1 hour; 4L: 4 hours; 7S: 7 hours
15. Workshop III: Focus group reviews overall experience and long term training projects. STO: 1.5; 4L: 6 hours; 7S: 10.5 hours

CONCLUSIONS

Implementation of an ILS presents great challenges and opportunities to the library administrator. In the rush to purchase, install and access an automated system, the administrator may easily overlook the importance of the comprehensive training program for staff. This program must be linked directly to the strategic planning process of the library and must be sensitive to obvious physical, fiscal, and human resource utilization limitations imposed by organizational constraints.

The FEA approach to problem identification and staff development strategies can help insure that the library administrator does not "jump" to invalid training solutions. Rather, he/she seeks to create a comprehensive plan with high-level support and staff-level involvement. It is also appropriate in any training effort so that the importance of proper ILS utilization is reinforced [15]. Finally, the administrator must understand that training demands a significant time commitment which changes (but does not evaporate) over time.

REFERENCES

1. William Saffady, "Characteristics and Experiences of Integrated Library Systems Installations," *Library Technology Reports* 23 (September-October 1987): 661.

2. Richard Boss "Annual Survey of Automated Library System Vendors—Turnkey Systems," *Library Systems Newsletter* 8 (March 1988): 17-24; "Software Only Vendors," *Library Systems Newsletter* 8 (April 1988): 25.

3. Ibid., p. 17

4. Saffady, p. 724.

5. Ibid, p. 758

6. Ibid, p. 759

7. Stuart Glogoff and James P. Flynn, "Developing a Systematic In-House Training Program for Integrated Library Systems," *College & Research Libraries* 48 (November 1987): 528-536.

8. Joseph Harless, *An Ounce of Analysis is Worth a Pound of Cure* (Newman, GA: Harless Performance Guild, Inc., 1975).

9. "Classics: Front-End Analysis," *Training* 24: (July 1988): 43-45.

10. Gary A. Rummler, *Human Performance Problems and Their Solutions*

(Ann Arbor, MI: University of Michigan Graduate Bureau of Industrial Relations, 1972).

11. Leonard Nadler, *Designing Training Programs: The Critical Events Model* (Reading, MA: Addison-Wesley Publishing Co., Inc., 1986), p. 19.

12. Ibid., p. 24.

13. For a look at the importance of developing a sound, highly supported training program, see the books and articles written by Martin Broadwell.

14. Kay Tytler Abella, *Building Successful Training Programs* (Reading, MA: Addison-Wesley Publishing Co., Inc., 1986) p. 127-130.

15. Nadler, p. 228.

APPENDIX

SAMPLE NEEDS ASSESSMENT:

Participant's Training, Background and Expectations

1. Have you been trained to use an automated systems?
   ___ Yes ___ No If yes, please indicate which system.

2. What type of training did you receive in order to work on that system? Check all that apply.

   ___ Trained by co-worker   ___ Programmed text
   ___ Trained by supervisor   ___ On-the-job training
   ___ Followed instructions   ___ Formal coursework
       in a manual
   ___ Computer assisted   ___ Vendor conducted
       instruction   workshop
   ___ Other _____

3. Did you feel that you needed a better background in library functions and automation in general for the training to have been more meaningful? ___ Yes ___ No If yes, explain what you would like to know.

4. Did you have sufficient opportunities to ask questions?
   ___ Yes ___ No If yes, were these questions asked
   ___ one-to-one or ___ in a group?

5. What did you consider the single best training technique (lecture, demonstrations, readings, hands-on experience, etc.).

6. How was the above training technique valuable to you in your everyday work?

7. What method(s) do you recommend not be included and why?

8. Is there a particular task you hope this training will enable you to do better? Please explain?

9. What do you suggest be done so that sufficient supervisory support will be forthcoming to enable a successful training environment?

10. Please use this section, the back of this page, or attach a sheet for additional comments.

<u>Administrative Team</u>

1. In your view, what is the most significant purpose associated with implementing the automated system?

2. What role should an in-house staff training program play in implementing the automated system?

3. Do you feel our current staff training methods are sufficient to ensure staff competence on the automated system?
    ___ Yes ___ No If not, which of the following new methods would you recommend?

    ___ training by co-workers   ___ training by supervisors
    ___ training manuals   ___ formal course work
    ___ vendor workshops   ___ hands-on training
    ___ other

4. As a result of training, what job skills or performance improvements would you hope to see among your staff?

5. What have been your experiences in training staff to use an automated system? Please explain in detail.

6. Would you be willing to assist in conducting in-service training programs?

7. Would you be willing to release members of your staff to assist in conducting in-service training programs? If yes, how many hours per week is reasonable?

8. How do you suggest we deal with anticipated drops in staff productivity during the training cycle?

    a. meeting client expectations
    b. handling daily job tasks within each unit
    c. interacting with other units

9. Please use this section, the back of this page, or attach a sheet for additional comments.

Training for Public Services

Elena E. Cevallos
Charles E. Kratz

SUMMARY. In-service training plays a pivotal role in the preparation of public services staff in libraries. This paper will define training and focus on the planning process necessary for the effective development and implementation of on-the-job training programs, including the goals of a training program, the general and specific behavioral objectives of a program, and the knowledge, skills, and abilities required by all public services positions for effective service within varied library environments. Part II of the paper will discuss the selection of appropriate training techniques and formats and concentrate on the use of video as a training tool and the practical training applications that have been developed within the library world and in other sectors. Video is a promising tool which should be utilized for training purposes.

INTRODUCTION

The training of public services professionals and support staff in today's library is a major task. A task made more difficult, and yet more essential, by the increasing application of computer technology in public services functions. The knowledge, skills, and abilities needed by public service staffs are likely to differ among libraries of varying types and sizes with diverse service goals and objectives. Additionally, no one agent is capable of providing all of the training required for quality public services in our libraries; rather, it is a responsibility shared by the library schools, the employing libraries, the employee, the professional organizations, and

---

Elena E. Cevallos is Reference/Coordinator of CD-ROM End-User Services at the Hofstra University Library, in Hempstead, NY.
Charles E. Kratz is Assistant Dean of Public Services at the Hofstra University Library, in Hempstead, NY.

© 1990 by The Haworth Press, Inc. All rights reserved.

consultants. The education for librarianship literature suggests that the issue of training is further complicated by the fact that each of these training agents has different perceptions of their responsibilities for training. As if this were not enough, survey research indicates that the individual being trained also has perceptions of what training should be provided by each agent.

Despite the enormity of the training task—managers spend 90 percent of their time concerned with personnel issues and problems,[1] the effective utilization of staff is a crucial management function within our libraries. The training of competent and effective public service staffs is critical to the perceived effectiveness of the library in carrying out its missions and goals. Recently, Professor Henrik Edelman of Rutgers University's School of Communication, Information & Library Studies observed that users' perceptions of the quality and effectiveness of the library, and user satisfaction with library services, are based primarily on user interaction with public service staffs.[2]

Personnel training contributes to other organizational and employee goals. First, it decreases the time needed to bring the new library employee to a satisfactory level of performance; second, it decreases the costs of managing the following activities: turnover, absenteeism, accidents, grievances, and complaints; third, and most significant, it decreases the costs of efficiently providing quality public services by improving the level of competency of those responsible for providing these services.

There is agreement that training is a necessity, but many questions still remain. What is meant by training, and what training activities are subsumed under the heading of training? Is there any commonality of skills and abilities which apply to both professional and support components of library public service staffs? How does one develop an effective training program? What techniques or strategies are available to provide training? Which formats hold the most promise as vehicles for training? What practical training applications have been developed within the library community and in other sectors which may be appropriate for the development and improvement of library public service staffs? This paper will focus on these issues and emphasize in-service or on-the-job training activities.

TRAINING DEFINED

There is no one definition of training. The simplest of these definitions states that the "singular function of training is to produce change in performance."[3] Paul Muchinsky views training as the "formal procedures which . . . [an institution] utilizes to facilitate learning so that the resultant behavior contributes to the attainment of the . . . [institution's] goals and objectives."[4] Sheila Creth's definition of training combines the two above definitions in a clear statement:[5]

> . . . the primary objective of . . . training is to bring about change—an increase in knowledge, the acquisition of a skill, or the development of confidence and good judgment . . . Training is not successful unless the person can do something new or different or demonstrate a change in behavior.

By definition, training is a broad rubric for other training related activities and programs, such as continuing education, formal education, in-service or on-the-job training, and staff development which lead to changes in performance behavior.

PUBLIC SERVICE STAFFS: REQUIREMENTS

What are the knowledge, skills, and abilities needed by library public services personnel to provide effective services to users? This question cannot be answered without being aware of the differences among the terms knowledge, skills, and abilities. Library administration needs a clear understanding of these concepts in order to develop appropriate training programs. Creth indicates that knowledge is the information needed to perform a set of activities well; skills are the techniques, methods, and strategies which put knowledge into practice; and abilities are intangible qualities such as cooperation, flexibility, motivation, enthusiasm, etc.[6]

Over and above the core knowledge imparted to professional librarians by the nation's library schools, employing libraries strongly emphasize Creth's abilities category for professionals, but these traits are equally applicable to public service support staff. In discussing the needs of medical libraries, Erika Love suggests that librarians should be team players; they should have intellectual curiosity, strong verbal and written communication skills, strong social/ interpersonal skills, enthusiasm, pride, self-esteem, and dynamism.[7] In addition to these often cited intangible traits, Karen K. Niemeyer emphasizes that a good media librarian should also be flexible, dedicated, honest, tactful, patient, and a leader. Media librarians should also have a sense of humor, an inclination toward public relations, listening skills, clarity of vision, a catalytic nature, stamina, and perseverance.[8] This impressive array of abilities are, in whole or in part, also found in discussions of professional personnel requirements in academic and public libraries.[9]

The need for these intangible but crucial qualities are supplemented by the expectation that public service staffs have specific skills as well. High on the list are organizational, management, and problem-solving/analytical skills. Equally important are various kinds of computer skills: online database searching, database management, automated systems expertise, word processing, etc. The increasing penetration of computer technology in libraries will lead to an accelerating demand for greater computer literacy among a broad range of library personnel.

Library professionals have their own opinions concerning where needed skills and abilities were learned. Three hundred and forty-nine ARL (Association of Research Libraries) librarians indicated that the following skills were acquired on the job, not in the library school: oral communication skills, knowledge of specialized reference sources, decision-making ability, search strategy, planning, online searching, selection of materials, personnel management, library automation, structure of subject literature, bibliographic instruction, and staff training and development.[10] Many of the skills cited by these librarians are emphasized by employing libraries as important for effective library service. In-service or on-the-job training programs have much to do.

TRAINING PROGRAM DEVELOPMENT: INTRODUCTION

The planning and implementation of a successful employee training program is not an easy undertaking. It requires rigorous analysis of training needs and a long-term investment of time and support by management to develop a program. Gary Mitchell identifies 13 issues which must be addressed, if a training program is to be successful:[11]

- A budget,
- Supervisory and management support,
- A tie-in to larger library efforts — missions, goals, etc.,
- A system for advertising the program,
- A rationale expressing the library's need for the program,
- A set of management goals,
- A plan for recruiting participants,
- A statement outlining the library population addressed by the program,
- Training objectives,
- A decision regarding who will deliver the program,
- A set of evaluation tools,
- A step-by step agenda that outlines when each element will be covered and how much time is allowed for it, and
- Training manuals and handouts.

The budget and administrative support are the most critical. If either or both of these items are missing, it will be impossible to develop or implement a successful employee training program. The impetus for such a program must come from the upper levels of library administration; library employee training must be an administrative priority supported with adequate resources, monetary and other, placed at the disposal of training program developers.

IN-SERVICE OR ON-THE-JOB TRAINING

In-service or on-the-job training programs are critical to the development of quality library services; Sheila Creth "believes that improved job training is an unrealized source for library effectiveness."[12] The significance of on-the-job training has been underscored by practicing librarians; Gemma DeVinney's and Patricia Tegler's survey of 54 SUNY (State University of New York) librarians concluded that most respondents considered on-the-job training as their most important means of learning job responsibilities, and 36 percent of those librarians for whom reference is a primary activity felt that on-the-job training was most important in preparing them for reference responsibilities.[13]

Closely allied to in-service or on-the-job training is staff development. Conroy defines staff development as

> a purposive effort intended to strengthen the library's capability to fulfill its mission effectively and efficiently by encouraging and providing for the growth of its human resources. Its general purpose is to assure that library personnel are motivated, productive, and skilled in their jobs, and that they understand and can implement library purposes and policies.[14]

From this definition, it is clear that in-service and on-the-job training are but components of the broader activity referred to as staff development.

The lack of or poorly designed job training programs leads to low library staff morale, and it breeds negative attitudes among the library staff about the library, the library staff itself, library administration, and the value of the work performed. When these negative attitudes are transmitted to the library user, it leads to user dissatisfaction.

There are numerous factors which contribute to inadequate in-service training. Understaffing in libraries means that public services desks must be covered as quickly as possible, even if the person is minimally or poorly trained; library management may often set a higher priority on having a "body at the desk" rather than on needed training; and, some library administrations may not adhere to "preventative, planned" approaches to management.[15]

Planning an On-the-Job Training Program

Planning, developing, and implementing an on-the-job training program is not for the faint hearted or those who are looking for a quick fix for personnel problems. The planning process is a long one which requires detailed analysis and appropriate decisions based on the analysis.

How do you begin the planning process? First, the knowledge, skills, and abilities required by all public services staff positions within a particular library environment must be identified. This first step is referred to as a job/function task analysis. The information required for the analysis is normally found in job descriptions which all libraries should have for both their professional and support staffs.

In addition to ascertaining the knowledge, skills, and abilities required by each position, library management needs to specify the percentage of time needed to perform various tasks, thereby setting priorities for employee performance. A decision must also be made concerning which task among the many performed by each employee are crucial to the ability of various public services departments to meet their service objectives. An important part of the last step is the setting of performance standards; a statement is required regarding performance expectations.

Once the job/function task analysis is completed, an organizational analysis is needed to determine within which public service areas training can and should be emphasized; further, a "person analysis"[16] will identify which individual employees need training and what training each employee needs. Armed with all of this information, objectives need to be written. Two kinds of objectives are required, first, a general statement concerning expected performance levels at the end of the training program; and second, training objectives for each unit within the training process.

Throughout the planning and implementation process, there should be constant evaluation and re-evaluation. Evaluation is taking place on several levels: the program as a whole, the individual participating in the program, and the influence of the program on the effectiveness of library's services.

Training Methods and Techniques

Once behavioral objectives for the training program are finalized, it is necessary to select the methods and techniques which will be utilized to train the staff. Generally, more than one strategy will be used to reach the objectives of the various units of the training program. There are a multitude of techniques available for training, each with its own strengths and weaknesses.

In the oldest and most common form of on-the-job training, established or senior co-workers instruct the employee. The employee learns the job by imitating the co-worker. Transfer of learning is maximized in this method; but training is brief and unstructured; the senior co-worker may find it a nuisance; and the employee being trained may be pressured to master the job too soon. In addition, the employee may learn to perform the job as their more senior colleague does, and this may not be the appropriate or most effective way of doing the job.

There are many positive features to the job rotation technique. It acquaints workers with many jobs within the institution which provides the employee with an overall view of the library's operation. For the organization, it creates a more flexible staff whose broad skills and abilities can be utilized where needed in the organization. However, effective job rotation takes an inordinate amount of time which many libraries may not have the luxury of setting aside for this method of training.

The lecture method is an often used teaching strategy. Its strength is that it can reach a large audience, and it can provide important general information effectively. As a training tool it has several weaknesses; it is a one-sided conversation without input from the learner, and it cannot easily or effectively impart specialized information well. A lecture does not usually provide practice, feedback, or transfer. There are variations of the lecture approach: lecture/discussion or lecture/hands-on sessions.

One of the newer methods of instruction is Programmed Instruction (PI). This method breaks each task into smaller units, and each unit builds upon the previous unit. Programmed Instruction can appear in a workbook format, so called learning machine, and, more recently, computer software programs. PI provides the trainee with immediate feedback; the systematic order of the material means that the presentation is complete; the trainee is an active learner because of the interactive nature of PI; the trainee can control the pace of the program and repeat, without embarrassment, difficult units until the material is understood. A major disadvantage is that PI is time consuming to prepare, and some tasks are difficult to break down into a systematic sequence because there may be several correct ways to perform the tasks.

Related to PI is the more current Computer-Assisted Instruction (CAI). The computer is a flexible training tool. Computerized training materials provide the trainee with individualized instruction; it reduces training time; and it standardizes training for all employees.

The trainee can work at his/her own pace, can begin and end a training session when convenient, and can start at the place in the program where he/she previously left off. Its major drawbacks are that it can be very expensive and time consuming to prepare. Finally, adequate software programs seem to lag behind the ability of the computer.

More recent techniques often used in business are those of simulation/games and role playing. The simulation attempts to represent a real-life scenario which manipulates selected critical components of the situation. Simulations seem to be a good training method for tasks requiring cognitive skills and decision making. Role playing is aimed at enhancing human relations and social interaction. It involves many people with assigned roles in the scenario to be enacted, and each participant is free to act out his/her role however he/she chooses. Role playing is often used to teach reference librarians the reference interview. It could also be used to train support staff to interact more effectively with patrons across any public service desk.

MEDIA TECHNOLOGY

Audiovisual materials represent popular and effective vehicles for training staff. Greg Kearsley states:[17]

> Technology is applied to training to improve the productivity of students and teachers. This includes: reduced training time, fewer training resources needed, increased student achievement, lower attrition rates, increased job proficiency, and increased student/teacher satisfaction.

These improvements will be dependent on the specific technology that is applied in the training program.

While the first use of media in training had its origins with 16mm films during the 1920's, the first extensive use of films and filmstrips was made by the U.S. military during World War II. The significant use of films in training during the war years contributed to its continued use as a method of training in the post-war years.[18] During the second half of the twentieth century, the rise of two new technologies—video and videodisc had major impact in the training field. Kearsley predicts that videocassettes and videodisc will soon replace 16mm films as tools for training staff.[19]

Video

Of all the audiovisual tools, video technology holds the most promise as a training technique; its flexibility allows it to be effectively combined with multiple training methods: PI, simulation/games, role playing, etc. It is particularly suited to recording employee's performance behavior which can be observed, reviewed and evaluated by both the supervisor and the employee to improve behavior.

Kearsley offers a persuasive argument for the use of videotape technology in training. Videotape can be used:[20]

> as a medium and as a teaching/learning tool. In the former, videotape is used to present pre-recorded content; in the latter, video is used to record and play back a "performance." . . . As a presentation medium, video serves as a replacement for film. As a tool, video opens up new possibilities for instruction that are not provided by any other medium.

Videodisc has a number of unique qualities in comparison to videotape. It can combine static and dynamic media (print, slides, audio, motion sequences) and store digital information (computer programs). Videodisc, because of its interactive nature, forms a bridge between audiovisual/film/video technology and computer/communications technology.[21]

An organization contemplating the use of video in its training programs has three basic options from which to choose: commercially produced videotapes; in-house productions prepared to present instructional information such as new employee orientations; and videotapes of extemporaneous performances, which are replayed immediately. The latter can be used for self analysis and critique.

Why Use Video in Training?

Why does video hold such promise as a training technique? Barbara Conroy offers several major reasons given by training practitioners:[22]

- Instruction through media is effective for learning:
  - provides a context short of direct experience but close enough to serve as a learning experience,
  - encourages active participation and interaction and provides reinforcement,
  - provides a point of reference from which to work with others in discussion or action,
  - provides innovative ideas,
  - provides faster training,
  - illustrates the standard of performance sought,
  - serves as role model and as motivational factor,
  - serves as an alternative in training methods.

- Instruction with media is cost effective:
  - often more economical; training packages can be purchased or rented in various price ranges,
  - often an inexpensive method for updating materials and keeping information current,
  - off-the-shelf products less expensive than in-house equivalents,

- Use of media offers strong advantages:
  - clear message with a personal impact,
  - concrete image and content emphasis,
  - on-tap expertise at minimal cost,
  - easily adaptable to various uses,
  - effective with an audience of any size,
  - convenient, replicable and usable often.

Planning for the Use of Video

The use of video in training is determined by the design of the overall training program. For successful use of video, there should be a training commitment from senior management, development of objectives based on identified training needs, feedback and rewards after the training, appropriate playback equipment and technical support, trainers who are experienced in the use of the equipment and software, and appropriate support materials.[23] Additionally, Conroy suggests that the use of video needs to be consistent with the training goals and objectives; video packages can be adapted to meet the needs of trainees; and video packages need to be evaluated to determine their usefulness.[24]

Once a trainer has decided on video technology for all or part of a training program, the trainer needs to evaluate the video-based training materials available on the market. Conroy provides a useful list of selection criteria when reviewing or previewing training packages,[25] while Robert Sullivan and Dennis Myers offer an excellent "Program Description Form" to use in describing a training program and a "Checklist of Video-based Training Materials" to use in assessing whether a training program meets identified training needs.[26] Conroy also has contributed a valuable resource guide of audiovisual materials for managers and trainers to use in selecting video.[27]

Off-the-shelf packages do not always meet the identified training needs. When this occurs, the trainer must plan and develop an appropriate in-house package. Various options exist, including hiring a media consultant to plan and develop a training video, or producing an in-house package with present staff, equipment, and budget.

As with other methods of training, the objective evaluation of video training is often forgotten. Video can provide very exciting and beneficial training possibilities, but it is of major importance to evaluate the contributions made to the learning process.

Effective Video Use: Training Videos for Social Interaction

The Library Video Network (LVN) is an excellent example of how libraries can pool their resources to produce videotapes for public services training purposes. LVN, a cooperative project of twelve Maryland county libraries, has produced several in-house training programs that can be used by public services staff. Libraries can request these tapes on a preview, rental, or purchase basis.

LVN was founded because of the common needs for locally produced video programs on topics such as staff training, public relations and other community programming. Several successful LVN training tapes for public service operations include: "If It Weren't for the Patron," which emphasizes the importance of good public service attitudes, "Who's First . . . You're Next," which discusses methods of operating an active reference desk, and "Sensitivity to the Disabled Patron" and "Volunteers Make the Difference," which addresses the topic of special patrons and library staffing with volunteers.

Two LVN videotapes were designed to promote staff discussion on the topic of implementing an automated circulation system: "Days Online," which discusses options for staff in working with the public during a conversion and "Online; or, How Do You Spell Relief," which describes for the computer novice some of the advantages of an automated system and provides an opportunity for discussion among staff concerning their own experiences working with a computer. The advantages of these tapes is that they are not filled with facts nor "how to's" but instead with open-ended situations. They were designed to promote discussion of role played situations and to reinforce positive attitudes.[28]

Another example of video use in training public services staff is the Moravian College Library's video training program for their circulation staff. This training program was developed to train new student circulation employees, to introduce the same material to all students participating in the training program, and to decrease the library staff's training time.[29]

Among in-house, video-based training programs, HERTIS, the polytechnic and college library network based at Hatfield Polytechnic, has developed some of the most innovative. The network provides regular in-service training sessions and courses for their 250 staff members. Two of the sessions provided for library assistants are concerned with interpersonal skills and handling awkward situations. The use of trigger videos was introduced because something more was needed than the available commercially produced training packages and role plays were often unpopular and need skilled handling. A trigger video is a series of short episodes which are used to trigger discussion on key issues.

The objective of a trigger is to involve the viewer in the situation and to challenge the viewer to make an immediate response. Philippa Dolphin, Sub-Librarian, Academic Services, Hatfield Polytechnic, produced 25 triggers for in-house training in HERTIS libraries. Episodes included interactions between librarians, staff, and users and particular management problems. A variety of issues were covered: the library's image, courtesy, professional jealousy, handling aggression, budget cutbacks, racism, and sexual harassment.

Triggers have been very successful. Each generate approximately a 30 minute discussion. Dolphin reports that "participants have cited an increased confidence in dealing with awkward situations at work and greater awareness of the implications of various types of response and behavior, as a result of the trigger sessions."[30]

Improving the performance and job satisfaction of a library's public service staff was the topic of a training program designed at Indiana University Northwest in Gary, Indiana. The program goals included developing the interpersonal skills needed for the effective operation of the circulation/reserve desk, communicating the staff's role in the operation of the library, teaching desirable behaviors in providing quality public service, and suggesting techniques and procedures for making jobs less stressful. Video was used to tape four job situations. The first script demonstrated inappropriate behaviors and responses to user problems while the second provided desirable behaviors and appropriate procedures. During the training session, trainees first viewed the job situations with the inappropriate behaviors; a discussion followed to determine what the staff member had done incorrectly. Subsequently, the participants viewed and discussed the four situations depicting the desirable behaviors. Role playing followed the discussion.[31]

A relevant and effective training program was produced in the non-library sector. The interactive video "Critical Incidents in Discipline" was used to simulate disciplinary confrontations that upper elementary and middle school teachers often experienced, and to allow for practice and discussion of possible behavior responses. Alan Evans states that a review of the interactive video literature indicates that it is an effective means of communication that can decrease study time and, in some cases, costs, as well as simulate human interactions and allow user response.[32] This is an excellent example of an application of videodisc technology for training purposes. This application also demonstrates the potential for an effective library application for improving the interaction of public services staff with users.

Effective Video Use: Training Videos for Automation

The implementation of automated systems has given rise to the use of video for training purposes. The Manchester Polytechnic Library, a multisite library service, went online with its circulation control subsystem (CIRCO) in 1982-83. During the implementation, the library staff recognized the need for a staff training package to introduce all aspects of the circulation system. Based on an analysis of training needs, the intent of the in-house video package was to provide effective and efficient training, decrease individual training time, improve the quality of training and training transfer, improve job performance, provide a more efficient service for users, and assist with training at other site libraries.[33]

Videotape was selected primarily because of its capability to demonstrate computer screen displays as well as the movement of the cursor and response time. Other advantages included that it could be shown when the system was down, that there was no computer time involved, that it would allow for individual and group training, and that it would be quick and easy to produce and easily updated if the CIRCO is upgraded. Staff also designed a workbook to use with the video to assist the participants. After training was complete, trainees were asked to complete an evaluation questionnaire. Feedback concerning the success of the training was also received from the workbook responses and subsequent job performance.[34]

Interactive video is easily adaptable to use in training for public services. The interactive video package, "Getting Started: An Introduction to Microcomputers for Librarians," was designed for librarians and library school students who have little or no previous experience with information technology. In this package trainees are introduced to the basic purposes for which computers can be utilized in libraries, and to criteria to assess a library's microcomputer needs. Additionally, types of software and criteria for the selection of software and hardware are provided. Nancy Hammond concludes that "there is considerable potential for the use of interactive video for staff training and user education in libraries."[35]

CONCLUSION

The development and implementation of in-service training programs are imperative for effective public services in libraries. Library administrators must place a high priority on and commit resources to on-the-job training for all library staff. Training for public services is provided in many settings; however, in-service training has a pivotal role in the preparation of public services staff. Research surveys among librarians indicate that many of the skills and abilities prized by employing libraries were acquired on the job, not in library schools or through continuing education programs. For support staff, the skills and abilities required for public service positions, with few exceptions, are learned solely on the job. Improperly trained public services staff will have considerable impact on a library's services. These employees are likely to be poorly motivated, ineffective, and to espouse negative attitudes about the library and its staff. It is also likely that service from poorly trained employees will eventually lead to user dissatisfaction, and ultimately to an erosion of user support for the library and its missions and goals.

The design and implementation of an on-the-job training program requires detailed analysis, planning, and constant evaluation. Planners need to know the overall goals of the training program, the general and specific behavioral objectives of the program, and, most important, the knowledge, skills, and abilities required by all public services positions for effective service within each library environment. This basic information is crucial for the selection of appropriate training formats and techniques, such as job rotation, apprentice training, lecture, programmed instruction (PI), computer-assisted instruction (CAI), simulation/role playing, and audio visual materials. The last category includes an array of techniques: film, filmstrips, slides, and videotape.

Among the various audiovisual techniques, video is an extremely valuable training tool which should be utilized to train library staff. It is versatile, flexible, an effective teacher, cost effective, and easily adaptable to specific training needs. In addition, video is an excellent means of providing trainees with immediate feedback, and an exceptional method for developing and enhancing social interaction skills, which are so critical to effective public services.

A review of the literature indicates that video is not being used sufficiently in library on-the-job training programs. Yet, the examples cited here show that effective library related programs are being and can be developed. The topics covered by these videotapes and videodiscs represent only part of what can be taught through the use of video. Technological advances will make it easier to adapt video to the specific training objectives of whatever information, skills, and abilities need to be taught. Developers of training programs should think creatively and be willing to experiment.

For libraries contemplating the development of an on-the-job training program with video components, the following publications are excellent resource guides: Barbara Conroy, *Learning Packaged to Go: A Directory and Guide to Staff Development and Training Packages* (Phoenix, Az.: The Oryx Press, 1983); Sheila D. Creth, *On-the-Job Training: Developing Library Resources* (Chicago: American Library Association, 1986); *Staff Development: A Practical Guide*, edited by Ann Grodzins Lipow (Chicago: Staff Development Committee, Personnel Administrative Section, Library Administration and Management Association, American Library Association, 1988); and *Training Marketplace Directory* (Minneapolis, Mn.: Lakewood Publications, Inc., 1988).

NOTES

1. Edward Evans, *Management Techniques for Librarians*, 2nd ed. (New York: Academic Press, 1983), p. 211.

2. Henrik Edelman, "Library Education for the New Academy: Views from the Field," *Futurists or Fossils: Librarians in the New Academy*, The Greater

Metropolitan New York Chapter of the Association of College and Research Libraries, Annual Symposium, November 18, 1988.

3. Gary Mitchell, *The Trainer's Handbook: The AMA Guide to Effective Training* (New York: American Management Association, 1987), p. 7.

4. Paul M. Muchinsky, *Psychology Applied to Work: An Introduction to Industrial and Organizational Psychology* 2nd ed. (Chicago: The Dorsey Press, 1987), p. 245.

5. Sheila D. Creth, *Effective On-the-Job Training: Developing Library Human Resources* (Chicago: American Library Association, 1986), p. 3.

6. Ibid.

7. Erika Love, "Medical Libraries" in *Education for Professional Librarians*, edited by Herbert W. White (White Plains, N.Y.: Knowledge Industry Publications, Inc., 1986), p. 113.

8. Karen K. Niemeyer, "School Libraries and Media Centers" in *Education for Professional Librarians*, edited by Herbert W. White (White Plains, N.Y.: Knowledge Industry Publications, Inc., 1986), pp. 123-124.

9. See Sheila D. Creth, "University Research Libraries" and Donald J. Sager, "Large Public Libraries" in *Education for Professional Librarians*, edited by Herbert W. White (White Plains, N.Y.: Knowledge Industry Publications, Inc., 1986), pp. 15-17, 38-40.

10. Ronald R. Powell, "Sources of Professional Knowledge for Academic Librarians," *College & Research Libraries* 49 (July, 1988):333.

11. Mitchell, p. 158.

12. Creth, *Effective On-the-Job Training: Developing Library Human Resources*, p. v.

13. Gemma DeVinney and Patricia Tegler, "Preparation for Academic Librarianship: A Survey," *College & Research Libraries* 44(3) (May, 1983):226.

14. Barbara Conroy, *Library Staff Development and Continuing Education* (Littleton, Colorado: Libraries Unlimited, Inc., 1978), p. xv.

15. Creth, *Effective On-The-Job Training: Developing Human Resources*, p. 10.

16. Muchinsky, p. 256.

17. Greg Kearsley, *Training and Technology: A Handbook for HRD Professionals* (Reading, MA: Addison-Wesley Publishing Co., 1984), p. 4.

18. Ibid., p. 29.

19. Ibid., p. 30.

20. Ibid., p. 34.

21. Ibid., p. 37-38.

22. Barbara Conroy, *Learning Packaged to Go: A Directory and Guide to Staff Development and Training Packages* (Phoenix, AZ: The Oryx Press, 1983), p. 3-5.

23. Kathy J. Coster and Lynne E. Bradley, "Video and Cable: Using Technology to Train about Technology," in *Training Issues in Changing Technology* (Chicago: Library Administration and Management Association, American Library Association, 1986), p. 64.

24. Conroy, *Learning Packaged to Go*, p. 13-14.
25. Ibid., p. 25-26.
26. Robert F. Sullivan and Dennis C. Myers, "Evaluating Video-Based Training Materials," *Training and Development Journal* 41 (June 1987), p. 82-83.
27. Conroy, *Learning Packaged to Go*, p. 40.
28. Coster and Bradley, *Training Issues*, p. 64-66 and Kathy J. Coster, "The Library Video Network: A Cooperative Approach for Videotaped Library Training Programs," *Public Libraries* 24 (Summer 1985), p. 78-79.
29. Gregory A. Crawford, "Training Student Employees by Videotape," *College & Research Libraries News* 49 (March 1988), p. 149-151.
30. Philippa Dolphin, "Interpersonal Skills Training for Library Staff," *Library Association Record* 88 (March 1986), p. 134.
31. Charles J. Hobson, Robert F. Moran & Arena L. Stevens, "Circulation/Reserve Desk Personnel Effectiveness," *Journal of Academic Librarianship* 13 (May 1987), p. 93-98.
32. Alan D. Evans, "Realistic Simulations for Teacher Training Using Interactive Video," *Ohio Media Spectrum* 39 (Spring 1987), p. 61-63.
33. Lynn Elliott, "CIRCO at Manchester Polytechnic Library: The Development of a Staff Training Package," *Audiovisual Librarian* 10 (Autumn 1984), p. 205-210.
34. Ibid.
35. Nancy Hammond, "Getting Started with Interactive Video," *Audiovisual Librarian* 13 (February 1987), p. 39 & 43; and Nancy Hammond, "Interactive Video for User Education and Staff Training—Less Expensive Than You Think," *Audiovisual Librarian* 14 (February 1988), p. 36-37.

Options in Learning: Instructor Led and Computer Based Training (CBT)

Janet L. Mushrush

SUMMARY. How well people learn, not how training is conducted is the measure of successful training. Prior to being able to decide on a class format, solid audience definition must be performed because expectations are critical to success. Once expectations are determined, the best way to transfer the needed knowledge and skills can be decided. This article discusses the differences between instructor led and computer based instruction for training.

Instructor led training is most valuable in conceptual training where adaptability and interaction are key. However, where computer or procedural skills are the desired outcome, Computer Based Training (CBT) is the preferred method.

When these two class formats are paired, an excellent method for transferring content is born. Trainees have the advantage of concepts presented by an instructor and the skills practice necessary for mastery of the procedure thru CBT.

Just as audience definition must be performed in the beginning, a class is not complete without evaluation and follow-up. This assists in continually improving the overall learning experience regardless of the format chosen.

In today's expanding environment of systems and management there are as many different approaches to training as there are classes to conduct. Fifteen years ago, if someone needed to learn a subject, they usually attended a class, took notes and then went back to the work place to go about the task of "doing." Sometimes

---

Janet L. Mushrush is Branch Manager for ComTech Systems, Inc. in Cincinnati, OH. She was formerly Director of Corporate Product Services for OCLC, Inc., in Dublin, OH.

© 1990 by The Haworth Press, Inc. All rights reserved.

a book was used for reference after class to supplement those topics introduced in class. Ten years ago, we began to see some hands-on practice in class that began to accelerate the learning that was happening mostly at the work place while trainees were "doing." Five years ago, computer-based training (CBT) entered the training arena in earnest, mostly addressing the PC software market: Lotus, DBase II, etc. In the years since companies have adopted CBT to handle almost 40% of their training needs, both for system-related procedures and general management practices. While there has been significant change in the ways systems and management are taught, the two things that haven't changed in at least 15 years are (1) people learn differently, and (2) people learn by "doing."

How well people learn, not how training is conducted, is the measure of successful training. Therefore, if people learn differently, those responsible for teaching must be able to accommodate those differences. Options are the answer. For the purpose of this article, this author will address CBT and instructor-led classes. However, prior to discussion of either method, we must look at the one area to which very little attention is paid, and can be the one which affects the learning process the most.

AUDIENCE DEFINITION

Before an instructor decides what format a class will need, he or she must perform the hardest task, defining the audience. Many training organizations attempt to provide guidelines in their literature to assist in determining who should attend. These guidelines are sometimes vague, but as audience definition is increasingly organized as a key to successful training, they are becoming more precise. One sees these in the "who should attend" section of brochures and some even get to the job title level with responsibilities included. But many times, the content does not necessarily match the advertisement, so people interested in sending staff don't always pay attention. Consequently, people end up attending who could not grasp the content due to its complexity or who are so advanced in the practices being presented that they are very difficult to instruct. The instructor will end up with low evaluations not because of anything he or she did; in fact the content may have been exactly what was advertised. Those who attended will go back to work, unsatisfied with the class, with the time and money they spent and, worst of all, without the knowledge they sought.

There is very little an instructor can do to alleviate this situation. An effective tool is a pre-class "profile" of each attendee that requests not only content-specific information but also asks each attendee to evaluate his or her own skill level. This practice is time consuming, and it's not fool-proof. Few training companies take the time and effort to do this; however, it is an excellent way for an instructor to familiarize him or herself with the attendees and what their expectations will be upon entering the class. Expectations, and not course content, instructor style, format or method is what makes or breaks a good learning experience.

Let's look at training via the first format: instructor-led.

INSTRUCTOR-LED TRAINING

Instructor-led training is the time-honored, tried and true method by which most training is handled. Its advantages are:

1. human interaction with trainees,
2. the ability to change the course content to adapt to the audience's skill level (adaptability), and
3. pacing of the learning time.

If trainees are slow to catch on to the topic, the instructor can slow the pace to ensure better content transfer. However, because people learn at different paces, those in the class who are learning more quickly are bored in the slow pace. With an instructor, trainees are able to ask the questions they need to transform information into knowledge, but those who have already learned it have probably tuned out, or moved ahead in the class materials.

On the other side of the pacing issue, if the class is particularly quick to catch on, the instructor will move at a pace to accommodate this. He or she may move to tips and short cuts to assist these faster learners. And since the instructor knows the topic better than anyone else, he or she is very well equipped to do this. However, this approach can sometimes leave out basic instruction the trainee may need when he or she returns to the work place to apply the training. While adaptability is a distinct advantage, it also jeopardizes the quality of the content. This is an especially important consideration when the topic is system oriented where the objective is to teach everyone the correct use of the application or the system. The instructor and his or her style also has a profound effect on the learning experience and on the decision to choose an instructor-led format for a class. Everyone who has ever attended classes, regardless of the content can remember both good and bad ones. These experiences can largely be attributed to the instructor. Human nature is such that the criteria for judging a good or bad instructor is not necessarily how well the class learned, but how the instructor related to the class and presented the material. In the arena of instructors there are many judged to be "good" who do little toward enhancing the learning of the trainee. Yet people will repeatedly attend classes by these instructors because of their reputations. Indeed, if organizations are setting up a training program, they will get a "name" as the draw in order to assure good attendance. While there is nothing wrong with this practice, instructor style should never be the sole criterion for judging quality of instruction or of learning. There are ways to lessen the impact of instructor style on selection of format for classes which will be discussed later in this article.

Stand-up instruction is a valuable option to be exercised in those areas where concepts predominate, rather than rote procedural skills, usually equated to "hands-on."

COMPUTER BASED TRAINING

Computer based training (CBT) has come to the forefront in the recent past as an excellent tool for training where computer skills are required. Its advantages are:

1. trainees learn at their own pace
2. trainees incur no travel expense, as it can be taken at the trainee's work place,

3. many trainees can use the same package once it is acquired,
4. trainees learn on the equipment they will be using daily, and,
5. trainees receive consistent content delivery.

Learning at the individual pace of the trainee is one of CBT's best attributes. CBT can be taken as many times as the trainee requires in order to learn the subject. Where repetition is the key to mastery of the skill, especially for system-related content, CBT is the format of choice. The instructor need not alter the pace of the class because the pace is dictated solely by each student. The trainees need never ask questions in class—their number one fear—and risk looking stupid in front of their peers. Learning new things is intimidating for most people. It most often requires change, the thing most frightening for most everyone above the age of 10. This is never more true than when learning new system practices. Instructors sometimes make the mistake of saying "this is easy" which plants the seed in the trainees mind that if they can't get it right the first time, there's something wrong with them. Computer based training makes no judgements about the ability of the trainee to learn. It doesn't know or care. It simply keeps instructing at the exact same level of instruction. The trainee is the only one who needs to know how he or she learned the content.

Associated Costs

No travel or class fee is required once CBT is chosen as the option for learning. In addition, many people can be trained with the same package. Cost benefits may be the single biggest consideration for use of CBT. Once the investment in CBT is made, initial training as well as on-going training can be accomplished. Three years ago, the attrition rate in libraries was 10%. For organizations experiencing attrition or turnover rates of anything higher than 2%, new hires can be trained on systems and products for no additional cost and little time taken from the job. That is not to say that upfront costs are not high.

Development Costs

For those organizations developing CBT in-house, the development costs are difficult to recoup except in those cases where large numbers of trainees are involved or where the shelf life of a product is longer than 2 years. Even after approximately 5 years of knowledge about authoring courses, the training industry is still having difficulty showing the exact time investment in development. This is due in part to varying skill levels of different authors and varying degrees of difficulty of the subjects being taught. As high as 200 and as low as 50 developmental hours-per-course-hour are numbers used to justify costs to create CBT. As an example, OCLC has chosen to use CBT as its primary tool for training its new system. Because of the enormity of the task and the fact that the system development effort is still in progress, exact development hours are not yet known. However, 3 years ago we estimated the high end of 200 hours per course hour because of relative low levels of programming skills of the authors at that time (OCLC had only 1 author then) and since has had the advantage of 4 additional staff and the experience of 3 years of creating courses as well as continual upgrading of these skill levels through continuing education. When these costs are spread over the approximately 38,000 users, the cost per student is estimated at less than $20.00. Costs for reproduction are in addition to this of course, but current training standards for cost per trainee average $300.00 per 2 day course. Shown above, the cost decreases each time additional people or new users take advantage of this already in-house course.

Another advantage of CBT is that trainees using it in the work place can learn the skills required on the very equipment they will be using each day to perform the actual work. Learning to use new computer systems can be intimidating, with the biggest fear being that of change. But some of that intimidation may come from the fear of the equipment itself. When the trainee learns on equipment which he or she will be using each day, the learning content is transferred much faster. Thus, the productivity experienced by each organization in a training situation is not as severe. However, we must remember that learning new things, regardless of training format, will still result in an initial drop in productivity. We must plan accordingly.

The remaining advantage of CBT is consistent delivery of content. As presented earlier, an instructor has the flexibility to present material as dictated by both his or her expertise and the expertise of the attendees. While this is advantageous for some topics, it is not for system-related learning situations, where the ability to perform tasks exactly as required is the *only* criterion for successful content transfer. Until software is commonplace that performs the way humans think, software is developed heirarchically and right and wrong answers are the only ones accepted. Little room for creative thinking exists in software use. CBT provides consistent, procedural instruction, totally independent of anything except correct use of the system. For a system where this is the training goal, CBT is the format best suited for the job.

OPTIONS

While these two approaches are specific to types of skills to be transferred, the way they are used presents the opportunity for options in learning. We have seen the ability to use these two methods to achieve good training results. However, these diverse methods can be paired to achieve even better results for the trainee's learning experience.

One format is to have an instructor present a short overview both of the system and of what the trainee will learn in a CBT session. Concepts can be presented in this way which will set the stage for more detailed instructions and procedures. For example, in the case of system-related topics, a presentation of the way the different segments of an application interact to achieve a specific result, followed by an explanation of the help system, provides an initial experience. Correct use of reference manuals and explanation of the unit text and prerequisites for CBT produces a well-rounded, instructor-led class. The trainee leaves the session with the CBT package and the focus for the instructor then turns to supporting the trainee when he or she is at the work place, usually by answering questions on the telephone.

A second method is to provide the CBT package to each trainee, and then conduct a session afterwards focused on answering questions. This is extremely productive in that attendees are on a more equal footing of knowledge and understanding. This is most effective in treating the problem of having the wrong attendees at the class. This allows the instructor to move to a somewhat different level of instruction: assisting the already knowledgeable trainees in adapting that knowledge to their environment. The most effective learning takes place when the trainees have the knowledge to tailor their new skills to the library's existing work flow.

EVALUATION

Often considered only as an afterthought, and therefore not very well planned, is the evaluation process. Evaluation is the only way a learning experience can be judged short of bringing the instructor to the work place to see the skills in practice. Traditional evaluation usually takes the form of asking the trainee to complete a questionnaire at the end of the class. It usually asks open-ended questions such as "what did you like best or least about the session," etc. This is effective in honing the design of the class. However, evaluations generally confuse content with instructional style which leaves very little room to correct the areas which may need it. It may be that the content is very good but the instructor or medium wasn't appropriate to convey it.

At OCLC, we use two evaluations; one for "mechanics" and one about the medium or instructor. We ask about use of the materials, format of the class, etc. We use a scale of 1-5 so that results are more easy to quantify. Suggestions for input in these areas are also requested. We then ask for the trainees to give their impressions of the instructor or media. For instructor-led, we ask questions such as: was the instructor well prepared, did the instructor know the material being presented, what was the environment for learning, etc. For media-based, we ask if it facilitated learning, in what areas did you have questions you couldn't get answered, how long did it take you to learn the material, did you do the entire course all at once or in separate sessions, etc. This approach allows modification or improvement of only the specific areas requiring change. This kind of evaluation also allows for the validation of the parts that are considered good so that those areas can be replicated in future designs of courses or classes.

As definitive as this approach is, evaluation by trainees of these two areas given only to the training provider falls short of the feedback that course designers and deliverers need to validate the training experience. These people must put in place tools and techniques that expand the number of people evaluating effectiveness of training. Colleagues and management are able to judge the trainees' ability to perform the tasks learned from the training and should give feedback on this to the training provider. The provider should also give a tool to the trainee to complete 3 months after course completion to ascertain both how well the trainee retained the content and the trainee's ability to tailor the content to the work environment. When this is accomplished, true evaluation is complete. As a result, modifications can be made that truly reflect the needs of trainees.

Instructor-led and CBT were conceived to be separate methods of information transfer and both are still excellent choices. Used separately, they present two approaches. Used in combination as described above, and coupled with solid audience definition and evaluation, the options expand to fit the growing need for trained and knowledgeable people in every profession.

Preparing for Library Leadership

Susan Jurow

SUMMARY. The task of finding and developing potential leaders from within the library profession requires an understanding of what a leader is, as well as the challenges that librarianship will face as it enters the twenty-first century. This article explores five fundamental leadership competencies: vision, communication, trust, risk-taking and empowerment and examines how individuals learn from personal and organizational experiences. It suggests ways of incorporating programs and activities into the workplace that support the development of leadership skills. If everyone within the library community assumes responsibility for recognizing untapped talent and providing developmental opportunities for it to mature, it will ensure that the library field has a pool of competent, confident, committed leaders for the future.

Many libraries today are engaging in strategic planning, scenario building, and other future-oriented exercises. They are trying to understand the future, so that they can prepare themselves with the right combination of skills and resources to meet its challenges. Leadership is one such resource, and the need to focus on its role within the library profession is critical.

As this article is being written, 18 of the 120 Association of Research Libraries (ARL) institutions are seeking or have recently sought new directors. Almost 25% of the ARL member libraries have changed directors in the last four years. When we examine these vacancies in key leadership positions, a number of questions arise. Does this constitute a crisis in library leadership? Does it result of simple demographics—a large group of anticipated retirements, or do some of these vacancies represent an inability to meet

---

Susan Jurow is Director of the Association of Research Libraries Office of Management Services.

© 1990 by The Haworth Press, Inc. All rights reserved.

the challenges of the changing library role within the university context?

More and more, we're seeing important institutions within our field, such as RLG and OCLC along with some large academic and research libraries, going outside the library profession to find their leaders. Our libraries already have many "non-library professionals" in upper-level administrative positions in areas such as systems and financial management.

The question we must ask is whether we lack the talent for leadership within the profession or whether the talent that exists is going untapped. I believe the answer is the latter. This article focuses on the competencies that will be needed by those who aspire to lead the library profession through the anticipated and unanticipated changes of the next decade and into the next century. It will explore how these individuals and the libraries for which they work can best manage their human resources to support the development of these leadership competencies.

I will begin by outlining current thinking on the concept of leadership and by highlighting some of the assumptions being made about our future. I will examine the competencies identified with leadership and how they might be incorporated into library settings. Finally, I will conclude with some thought on the responsibility for leadership training and development in libraries.

LEADERSHIP

The debate continues on where and how we find leaders. There is a body of literature on the study of leadership which explores whether leaders are born or made, whether leadership is a collection of traits that a person has or whether leaders emerge from a unique situation or circumstance. An overview of this discussion can be found in many management textbooks (1) or management handbooks (2).

For the purposes of this article, I would like to focus on the recent work done by Bennis and Nanus (3) and Kouzes and Posner (4) and on the conceptual model that has resulted from their research. The methodology used by both sets of researchers includes interviews with and observation of acknowledged leaders, as well as discussions with their peers, associates, subordinates and bosses. They examined what characteristics these individuals displayed that lead others to recognize them as leaders and how these characteristics manifested themselves.

Although described in different words, both studies identify five strategies employed by these individuals: vision, communication, trust, risk, and empowerment.

Vision

The ability to see or to imagine a future that goes beyond what others believe possible was a primary characteristic of the individuals identified by these two groups of researchers. The direction their enterprise should take and the view of what the best possible future should look like was crystal clear. The compelling nature of their vision provided a hook on which others could hang their commitment, their loyalty, and their own sense of purpose.

Communication

The capacity to envision a unique image of an ideal future is crucial to leadership but meaningless without the ability to communicate that vision. So much of what is truly innovative and has the potential to reshape our views is lost through an inability to be articulate, to fire the imagination of others. The leaders in this study were those who were able to get the people around them to commit to and support their vision.

Trust

A high level of trust is needed to take individuals and an enterprise through an ambiguous period of transition into an uncertain future. One way that leaders are able to inspire others to do new things or act in unaccustomed ways for a greater good is by modeling a particular set of behaviors themselves. Individuals reported that part of their willingness to follow their leader in new directions was derived from his or her demonstrated personal commitment to a goal through consistent, personal efforts.

Risk

Leaders are also identified by others as those who challenge the status quo, experiment, and take risks. This does not seem to come as much from a desire for excitement as from a desire to learn. Learning is seen as a requirement for growth and change. The leaders in these two studies showed a bias towards action and viewed the mistakes they made and those made by others as part of the learning process.

Empowerment

Partly a strategy in itself and partly the logical result of the other four strategies, individuals around these described leaders felt strengthened by his or her actions and through his or her presence. When leaders create a vision that is a true reflection of the values, needs, and desires of those they intend to lead, their followers feel supported on a very deep level. They are more able to commit to and work toward the goals that have been articulated. They feel challenged and derive a greater sense of meaning from their work.

In combination, these five strategies provide us with a model for understanding leadership. One of its strengths is that it makes sense. Some of us watch leadership from afar as it operates in society at large. Others have been lucky enough to work with a true leader and have been able to observe these actions close at hand. For most of us, this conceptual framework matches with our personal experience.

The question still remains as to whether individuals armed with these strategies can provide libraries with the kind of leadership that will be needed to take them into the twenty-first century. To answer this, a better understanding of our anticipated future is required.

THE FUTURE

We look around and we can all see changes and trends that will have an impact on the way we operate both personally and professionally in the future. Gareth Morgan (5) and Joseph Johnston Jr. (6) have identified a number of these trends from which I have chosen those that I believe have the greatest relevance for libraries.

An Increasingly Turbulent Environment

Other eras have experienced enormous changes brought on by social, economic and technological developments. The difference today is that, along with the complex and large-scale character of the changes facing us, the rapid rate and ongoing nature of these change processes leave us with a sense of constantly being in a state of flux or transition.

Libraries will have to be prepared to add and eliminate services and technologies as need and demand shift. Library organizations were designed to produce a consistent, quality product — retrievable materials. Our structures will have to be revamped to permit us to be more responsive to these shifts.

An Information-Based, Service-Oriented Society

Libraries have always been in the business of collecting, organizing and facilitating access to knowledge. The information explosion has already had an enormous impact on the ability of libraries to maintain these traditional functions. We must prepare ourselves as society refocuses its attention and energy into an area that has traditionally been our private domain. We have always seen information as an inexhaustible resource. More and more, we are hearing it described and used as a commodity.

The Desire to Maintain Quality

We expect and our clients expect that libraries will continue to offer the same, high quality services that have been offered in the past. The quandary arises when opportunities for new or improved service present themselves. With little or no more money being added to base budgets, it is difficult to see how new programs can be created and the same standards of quality maintained.

Expectations of Shared Responsibility

A larger number of groups or individuals are being recognized as having a stake in the success or failure of an enterprise's endeavors. They can include the staff, the clients, and the suppliers. Organizations are beginning to learn to exploit their commitment by giving them a larger role in the functioning of the organization.

In libraries, we find staff want to be more involved in decisions that will affect the quality of their work life. Libraries are looking to publishers to recognize the partnership in which we're engaged in order to be more influential in the choice of paper used in book publishing or the price of serials.

More Complex Organizations

The changing nature of work and the decentralization of power has lead to organizations that are less hierarchical. The increased interdependence of the various units requires a greater emphasis on collaboration and a need for more and better communication structures.

The use of groups in the management processes of libraries has grown phenomenally over the past fifteen years. Traditionally, the role of the middle manager was to pass information up and down through the organization. With increased access to information at all levels through local computer systems, organizational structures are likely to continue to flatten.

Different Problem-Solving Requirements

The problems that face libraries now and that will confront them in the future will continue to grow more complex. They will require a variety of perspectives to understand and solve them, involving more people in the process. As the choices grow more difficult to make, a greater willingness to take risks will be necessary to avoid paralysis and to develop the kinds of innovative solutions that will be needed. Most library reward systems do not currently support these needs. By focusing only on successful completion of tasks, they discourage attempts to try new approaches which traditionally have greater potential for failure.

The Need for a Proactive Approach

By developing our ability to understand and anticipate the future through the analysis of current trends, we also enhance our ability to influence the future. Organizations can no longer afford to merely manage what happens to them. They have a responsibility to increase their effectiveness by trying to shape and influence the elements within their environment.

From these projections, we can begin to develop a picture of the kinds of knowledge or skills our leaders will need in order to meet these challenges. First and foremost is the ability to deal with ambiguity, to function effectively in situations where the rules and boundaries are not clear. Because there will be so few anchors, the ability to make choices and focus energy, (one's own and that of others,) will also be important.

Most efforts will be collaborative, rather than individual. An understanding of group dynamics and strong interpersonal skills will be essential to effective functioning. These group activities and the multiple constituencies we anticipate will make the ability to communicate clearly critical to personal and organizational success.

The leaders the library profession will need in the future must be able to employ the same strategies identified by the leadership studies already mentioned. Because of the ambiguous, uncertain nature of the future that we face, we will need leaders who are willing to take some risks and try new things. One of those risks will be making a commitment to a particular course of action and focusing the energy of an entire enterprise on the accomplishment of that goal.

In order to do that, our leaders will have to share their vision; they will need to communicate effectively their sense of purpose to others. They must possess both a good knowledge of individuals and groups and an understanding of what motivates them to make their best efforts. Our leaders will have to know how to tap into the strengths of others and how to build on those strengths. They need to make people feel uplifted, not diminished, by their commitment to an enterprise, a course of action, and a vision of the future.

LEARNING TO BE LEADERS

There are three issues to be considered in leadership training: what needs to be learned, where it should be learned, and how it should be learned. In the second part of this article, I will focus on specific competencies of leadership and how they might be nurtured within a library organization.

If we examine current research on how individuals become effective managers, we can find clues that will help us to develop models for effective leadership training in libraries. Some of this work has been undertaken by the Center for Creative Leadership (CCL) in Greensboro, North Carolina. By examining life histories, researchers at CCL were able to identify four arenas that play a major role in the development of successful, high-level executives. They were challenging assignments, other people, hardships and significant events.(7)

Challenging assignments included starting something from scratch, cleaning up a messy situation, taking on a project or being a part of a task force team, increasing responsibility, and switching from a line to a staff position. There were two ways in which other people had an impact on the development of these individuals: both negative and positive role models were identified; and memorable events of short duration, both positive and negative, demonstrating the impact of interpersonal interactions were described.

The kinds of hardships identified by the CCL study were errors in judgment or mistakes that led to failure, problem staff, having to starting over in a new job or career, and personal traumas. They also included career crises, such as demotions, being passed over for promotion, and lousy jobs — specifically, a job that was different from what was anticipated or desired. Other significant events included courses and formal training programs, early work experiences, (especially first supervisory experiences,) and an array of personal experiences that took place outside of the work environment.

The CCL study sought to discover how these executives learned to be effective or discovered an ability to be effective through these experiences. Participants in the study identified the lessons they believed they learned from these events (Figure 1). The lessons were clustered, then correlated with the appropriate event to see which experience seemed to have the greatest impact on the learning of a particular lesson.

FIGURE 1. Lessons from Experience

1. Direct and Motivate
2. Basic Management Values
3. Self-Confidence
4. Specific Technical Knowledge
5. How the Business Works
6. Dealing with People
7. Comfort with Ambiguity, Stress and Uncertainty
8. Politics is Part of Organizational Life
9. Getting Lateral Cooperation
10. Standing Alone
11. Human Values: Sensitivity to Human Needs
12. Persevering under Adverse Conditions: Singleness of Purpose
13. How to Work with Executives
14. Recognition of Personal Limits and Weaknesses
15. Seeing Organization as Systems
16. Learning to be Tough: Biting the Bullet, Do What Has to be Done Despite Consequences – to *another* person
17. Finding Alternatives in Solving and Framing Problems
18. Strategy and Tactics of Negotiation with External Parties
19. Needing to Act on or Confront a Subordinate Performance Problem
20. Strategies for Coping with Situations Beyond Your Control
21. Discovering What You Really Want to Do
22. You Have to Take Control of Your Own Career
23. What Executives are Like
24. Management is Different from Technical; People are Important and Problematic
25. How to Build and/or Use Structure and Control Systems
26. Develop Your People
27. How to Manage People Who Have More Experience Than You or Who Used to be Your Peer or Boss
28. Perspective on Life and Work
29. Dealing with Conflict
30. Can't Manage it All by Yourself
31. Be Ready to Take Opportunities
32. Use and Abuse of Power, Comfort with Power
33. Management Models
34. Doing it is More Important than Thinking about it – Practice over Theory

Source: Esther H. Lindsey, Virginia Homes, Morgan W. McCall, Jr. *Key Events in Executives' Lives*. Technical Report Number 32. Greensboro, NC: Center for Creative Leadership, 1987.

We have already identified the strategies connected with leadership behavior. Let us now explore the relationship between what these executives felt they learned from their experiences and what we want our leaders to know or know how to do.

DEVELOPING LEADERSHIP COMPETENCIES

Part of the utility of CCL's study is that it helps us to analyze how the competencies that lie behind the leadership strategies could be consciously developed. If we can identify at least some of the components that support an individual's ability to behave in a desired way, then we can develop activities that will enhance that ability.

Developing Visionary Potential

The ability to focus purpose into a unique, meaningful vision that can be acted upon is the characteristic most often identified with leaders. In many ways this is very similar to what the CCL study called setting and implementing agendas. Four of the lessons related to this quality would be useful in developing visionary potential: knowledge of technical/professional content, understanding how the business works, strategic thinking, and innovative problem-solving methods.

Moving from a line to a staff position was the experience that had the biggest impact on learning in these four areas. It helped the individual to develop a greater appreciation for other areas within their organization. Staff were also able to develop skills, such as planning, financial analysis, and human resources development that encourage and support a broader perspective. Outside coursework was also useful in supporting the development of technical or professional knowledge.

If we wish to construct developmental activities such as these in libraries, there are some key elements to build in and some to avoid. An effective staff assignment should be relatively short, about a year, and involve some form of organizational analysis to encourage abstract thinking.

Strategic planning is ideal, but projects that focus on financial analysis or program development could serve the same purpose.

During this process, the individual should report to someone higher up in the organization. This special reporting relationship makes the experience more meaningful by providing access to feedback that is broader in nature and gives the individual a greater sense of contribution. Routine jobs in personnel and administration do not provide the same kind of developmental growth.

Two other experiences that support growth in this arena are opportunities to start something from scratch and to fix something that's gone awry. As technology changes what is done in libraries and how it is done, we have more opportunities to provide start-up projects for those identified as having leadership potential. Developing new services for the public and new internal processes and procedures fit into this category. The critical elements are that the individual take full responsibility for the success or failure of the operation and that they work through the constraints and the pressures on their own.

There are always areas in our libraries that are not working as productively or efficiently as possible, and sometimes there are areas that need a complete overhaul. Rather than allowing these units to languish, the situation can provide an excellent opportunity to develop diagnostic skills and abilities. Individuals engaged in these kinds of undertakings learn the importance of careful analysis before action.

It seems that most of our approaches to problem-solving are developed during our earliest work experiences. Libraries that wish to encourage innovative thinking can assist staff by offering training in creative problem-solving techniques. These techniques can be institutionalized through effective meeting planning and their use encouraged throughout the organization.

Developing the Ability to Enlist Others

Kouzes and Posner (8) report that, based on their study of leadership, "inspiration" is the most difficult competency to learn. If we approach it from a pragmatic point of view, this issue relates most closely to communication and influencing skills. In the CCL study, the sections which dealt with handling relationships contain some data on influencing, but communication is not directly addressed.

Getting others to implement your solutions was most often learned from the earliest supervisory experience. The lesson was that in working with people, the people themselves are the key to success.

There are many projects in libraries that require "buy-in" by multiple constituencies, such as reorganizations, bringing up an online catalog, introduction of fees for services, and changes in performance evaluation systems. These kinds of assignments provide opportunities for potential leaders to make the connection between their ability to communicate the importance and benefits of an endeavor and its successful outcome.

The most critical step in the process of enlisting the support of others is understanding the group or groups with which one is working. In order to be convincing, one must know what ideas and ideals are held in common. In order to tap into these commonalities, we must know their values, what they believe in. The need for an analytical approach must be continually underscored.

We have all seen situations where a project was undermined because the appropriate level of energy and commitment had not been elicited from those who had to make the operational effort. Potential leaders must learn how and what advance preparations need to be made to ensure a successful change operation. If we want staff to develop in this area, we must give them feedback on their communication strategies, rather than evaluating them simply on the content.

We should provide critical feedback in terms of the mechanics of the communication process. The message should be repeated a number of times, in different ways, so that as many people as possible can be reached in as many different ways as possible. Examples of what the new approach has to offer should be credible and vivid, positive and hopeful, and passionate. People want to succeed and want the organizations for which they work to be successful. All forms of formal and informal communication should make them feel included in the vision. Formal and informal courses can also aid in the development of effective oral and written communication skills.

Developing Confidence and Encouraging Trust

The trust of others and self-confidence go hand in hand. It is difficult for others to trust us and have confidence in us if we do not have confidence in ourselves. How did the participants in the CCL study think that they developed confidence?

Surprisingly, the mechanism most often mentioned was coursework, with participation in projects and task forces a close second. Through courses, individuals are exposed to information and experiences not available in the workplace. The knowledge should be both conceptual and technical in nature. Classes also provide opportunities for self-assessment: sorting out personal strengths and weaknesses, as well as objective comparison with others. Supporting coursework through release time and direct financial aid is a way for organizations to show their support for individual development.

Projects and task force assignments provide the same kind of proving ground that formal coursework offers and can be designed to deliver a high level of developmental impact. A tight time frame forces staff to get up to speed quickly. The small group size ties the success and failure more closely to the individuals working on the project. If the project requires dealing with a variety of groups, the team members learn not only to coordinate their work with each other, but to negotiate relationships with those outside the group, as well.

Bennis and Nanus (9) also identify visible, tangible personal commitment to an idea or project as one of the elements that leads people to trust a leader. In CCL's study, the lesson of singleness of purpose and standing up for one's beliefs were most often derived from adverse conditions or situations.

Developing Risk Taking Potential

Risk is defined as the exposure to a chance of loss. Our ability to take risks comes in part from our desire to do something different or in a different way, recognizing and seizing opportunities, and having the confidence to stand alone and act. As described earlier, learning to find alternatives in solving and framing problems seems to come mostly from early work experiences.

Taking full responsibility was also one of the lessons learned through setting and implementing agendas. Participants felt they learned it from all their experiences, but most often it was learned in the process of cleaning up a mess and starting something from scratch. Decision making was the skill they felt they'd acquired, and a bias for action was the attitude that went with it.

Being prepared to take advantage of the unexpected was learned from difficult situations that forced the individual to exchange the known for the unknown. Situations that could foster this lesson are those that encourage an individual to move from an area with which he or she is comfortable and familiar, into an area where they do not have the same level of expertise. We do not take nearly as much advantage of job exchange programs as we could in this regard. A successful outcome will support independent risk taking in the future.

No one wants to fail or to see others fail. One of the problems with developing risk taking potential is that, in trying to protect ourselves and others from failure, we often become overly cautious and conservative in our approach. Even with all our precautions, each of us at some point in the past has made a mistake, missed an opportunity, or been the victim of unfortunate circumstances.

How the organization deals with these kinds of situations is the key to what learning is acquired from them. The lesson can be "don't ever try that or anything like that again until you're sure," or it can be "let's find out why that didn't work, so that we can try something else that might."

Developing Empowerment Skills

Rosabeth Kanter (10) has described empowerment as a process that makes power widely accessible within an organization. Her studies have shown that organizations which support this element as part of their culture produce more innovation (11). The power tools she describes are information, resources and support. A leader can only empower others to the degree to which he or she is willing to share these commodities.

Some of those who reported about their experiences in the CCL study learned lessons that apply to the development of this competency. These include politics as a part of organizational life, the use and abuse of power, discovering that a single person cannot do it all alone, understanding the perspective of others, and finding out how to develop others. Almost all of these lessons were reported to have come from hardship experiences, from failures, demotions, and personal trauma. To a lesser degree, increased responsibility also contributed to these learnings.

There are few who would argue that we should create situations for people to fail, so that they could derive the appropriate lessons from them. The critical factor in dealing with these experiences is learning how to learn from them. Postmortems are routinely done when someone dies, not to find fault, but to understand why it happened. There are many lessons to be learned when something does not go as expected or hoped.

We do not wish to stifle the individual creativity and initiative that leads to vision and risk taking in the process of developing empowerment skills. We do, however, want to find ways to help our potential leaders recognize that others have the same desire to contribute as they do. As can be seen from CCL's study, one of the most poignant ways that individuals learn this lesson is by trying to do things alone and failing. The true failure is in not recognizing the potential of others.

Kouzes and Posner claim to have developed a "simple one-word test to detect whether someone is on the road to becoming a leader. That word is *we*." (12)

CONCLUSION

Where and how do we find people who have all these skills? We need them now to influence our choice of direction and to help us find the energy and enthusiasm to take on the challenges that we face. The books tell us that leadership is not the charismatic, seldom seen phenomenon we once thought it to be. They say that leadership potential is spread throughout our organizations from the top to the bottom and that all we need to do is identify it and develop it.

If we want to have these people at the top, the investment in this development is going to have to be much larger than it has been. The numbers alone are against us. We are a very small profession, and the staff of large academic and research libraries make up a very small subset of that profession. Programs that attempt to assess leadership potential and focus on a few individuals are not going to have the kind of impact that is needed.

We need programs that are broader in scope. We need to provide opportunities for growth and development for more people, so that the potential leaders that are out there can grow into the roles and positions that are waiting for them.

Responsibility for these programs falls to all of us. As individuals we must explore and exercise the leadership potential within us and to nurture it when we see it in others. Libraries have a responsibility to create opportunities for leadership potential to flourish. Our professional associations can help by designing and delivering substantive skill building programs that support the organizational endeavors. Foundations can help by investing in broad-based development programs designed to uncover leadership potential.

These leaders will be needed in the coming years to help us look beyond our parochial interests and tie our actions to broader goals that lead to greater accomplishments. These individuals represent the most important resources of libraries today—our human resources. Leaders need to be nurtured and encouraged, so that they can fulfill their own potential and help our organizations fulfill theirs.

NOTES

1. Most management texts devote a chapter or section to the subject of leadership. Andrew D. Szilagyi Jr. and Marc J. Wallace Jr. *Organizational Behavior and Performance*, (Glenview, IL: Scott, Foresman and Co., 1983) covers recent research and has an interesting bibliography.

2. The best review of the topic can be found in Ralph M. Stogdill, *Handbook of Leadership*, (New York: Free Press, 1974), but a good overview of the issues from a human resources management point of view is that of William J. Thomas, "Leadership" in *Human Resources Management and Development Handbook*, ed. William R. Tracey, (New York: AMACOM, 1985).

3. Warren Bennis and Burt Nanus. *Leaders: The Strategies for Taking Charge*. New York: Harper & Row, 1985.

4. James M. Kouzes and Barry Z. Posner. *The Leadership Challenge: How to Get Extraordinary Things Done in Organizations*. San Francisco: Jossey-Bass, 1987.

5. Gareth Morgan. *Riding the Waves of Change: Developing Managerial Competencies for a Turbulent World*. San Francisco: Jossey-Bass, 1988.

6. Joseph S. Johnston Jr. "Educating Managers for Change," in *Educating Managers: Executive Effectiveness through Liberal Learning*, ed. Joseph S. Johnston Jr. and Associates. San Francisco: Jossey-Bass, 1986.

7. The most detailed account of the research study in Esther H. Lindsey, Virginia Homes and Morgan W. McCall Jr. *"Key Events in Executives' Lives."* Technical Report 32. Greensboro, NC: Center for Creative Leadership, 1987.

8. Kouzes and Posner, *The Leadership Challenge*, 109.

9. Bennis and Nanus, *Leaders*, 108.

10. Rosabeth Moss Kanter. *The Change Masters: Innovation for Productivity in the American Corporation*, (New York: Simon and Schuster, 1983.) 156.

11. Ibid., 159.

12. Kouzes and Posner, *The Leadership Challenge*, 10.

Training Endusers/Remote Users

Joe Jaros

SUMMARY. The advent of new technology has changed the teaching role of librarians. The increased role of enduser searching in academic libraries has meant that library instruction is now more important that ever. The experiences of Texas A&M University are examined as an example of a variety of teaching methods employed by one university library to meet the increased demands of its patrons for better enduser searches. Librarians, concerned over inadequate search strategies employed by patrons, design individualized instructions for a variety of databases, provide some individual, one-to-one instruction and teach in group situations employing equipment that allows onscreen projection from a monitor. Remote users have been trained to use the online catalog by development of a specialized training manual.

INTRODUCTION

The advent of new technologies has changed the traditional role of librarians as the purveyors of access to information. This in itself is nothing new, nothing remarkable, but what has changed alongside the advance of technology has been the change in the teaching format traditionally associated with reference librarians. Previously regarded as an aid, or transmitter of information, most reference librarians probably also considered themselves as teachers or educators. They believed that they frequently taught the user how to locate his/her information needs by illustrating the necessary procedures and tools used in the reference process, and then leaving the patron to find his or her requirements. This concept was probably more viable among academic librarians, bound within the tradi-

---

Joe Jaros is Head of Instructional Services at Texas A&M University, in College Station, TX.

tional learning setting, often dealing with a limited time frame as well as a limited staff. The truth may have differed from this self perception on the part of librarians, as most patrons probably remained concerned with the end product, i.e., their research needs, and not with the procedures required to attain them. In short, while the patrons may have learned the necessary procedures and tools within a particular instance, the likelihood was great that they would soon forget it and upon their next instance of need, they would return to the librarian with similar requests. If this is teaching, it often appears to the librarian that it is an educational process tinged with failure. Librarians find themselves teaching the same subject over and over to the same students, a relentless remedial process.

There also have traditionally been some library patrons who emphatically did not wish to learn anything remotely concerned with the reference research process. They regarded this as the librarian's responsibility and the latter's task was to simply furnish the user with the required information. Academic librarians have often encountered this type of belief on the part of their teaching and research faculty colleagues, but it is sure to be apparent in any library setting. The ideal college/university environment may be one wherein the learning-teaching process is a continual one, effecting all facets of academic life. Most academicians, however, are always leery of anything that might appear to concern "teaching" each other. After all, such is the reason for the existence of the student population and few faculty (including librarians) welcome being in a position requiring instruction from their colleagues.

Doubtless, similarities exist in many different types of library environments. Patron expectations and perceptions of the librarian's role differ from that of the professional. Few library users would probably regard the librarian as a teacher.

IMPACT OF TECHNOLOGICAL CHANGE

Technology, however, has caught up with all of us and the advent of the computer, the microchip and readily available databases have changed the structure of the information process. As librarians and information specialists, we have been told this many times in recent years. The fact remains, however, that the new technical advances regarding data storage, retrieval and manipulation have changed the duties of librarians and are probably changing the relationship between library patron and librarian. As technological advances increase, and as the cost of implementation of these advances lessen, more and more library users are going to come into contact with automated retrieval in some form or another.

When library patrons first encountered automated retrieval of information, it was probably in the form of a mediated search, the situation whereby the librarian, as a trained search analyst, conducted a database search and provided the patron with a bibliography of citations on his/her subject. This type of situation certainly confirmed the traditional role of the librarian as a purveyor of information, a means of access to assist the library patron in research needs. Such database searches did not even require the library user to be present, although many libraries have preferred the user to be there while the search was conducted and peruse the results online. Nonetheless, the situation was an ideal one to the "non-teaching" concept of the librarian's role. It exactly fit the traditional pattern whereby the user made a request for information and the librarian supplied him or her with their needs. The only apparent change that might be perceived by the user was the speed with which the answer was supplied, the depth of coverage and the monetary cost. It was quickly apparent that information was no longer necessarily free at the library, one had to pay for it if you wanted it fast and if you wanted to be fairly sure that the majority of sources had been adequately covered. In some ways, this has allowed the librarian to continue the mystique of the traditional "Keepers of Information" role, holders of the keys of access and the only ones who could answer their patrons needs. It was not necessary to teach the patron anything, although most librarians probably went through a fairly lengthy explanation as to what a database was, searching fundamentals, what one could and couldn't do in such a search, giving a factual description of what they were doing in accessing this type of information. The question remains, of course, as to whether the patron cared or not. In any event, he/she was furnished with their information needs and went on their way.

Enduser searching, however, has presented a new complexity to the situation and required a restoration of the teaching function for librarians. The situation of patrons doing their own searching brings to the forefront the question of how best to train the library user to retrieve his/her information needs. As more and more institutions allow enduser searching in online or ondisk systems, certain questions arise. No matter how user friendly a system may appear, most patrons are going to need some assistance simply to relate to the machine and to construct a search strategy that will enable them to get results, much less get the best results. The question remains how to best do this, given the available resources in finances and time.

THE TEXAS A&M EXPERIENCE

Texas A&M began an extensive enduser service in the fall of 1984, when it began offering BRS AfterDark on a limited, "first come, first served" basis from 6 p.m. until 10 p.m. during weekdays and from 9 a.m. until 6 p.m. on Saturdays. Soon they had to evolve a system whereby reservations were taken during the day for each evening and on Fridays for weekends. Within a few months, additional terminals were placed which allowed the use of four terminals each evening. Appointments were taken at 30 minute intervals, with each patron allowed approximately 20 minutes of online time. Reservations were taken in advance and allowed each individual to have a minimum of two searches per week. By 1986, about 4,300 searches a year were being run at an approximate cost of $5.67 per search.[1] In 1987, the Former Students Association began to give subsidies for student searches to allow for free connect time. Students then were able to have a search and only pay a minimal charge for prints. Since the library was also allowing searches in Knowledge Index with no print charges, they were able to offer many students , depending upon the availability of their database in a particular system, a free search. Current statistics show that over 64 searches are being done each week.

Also in 1987, through the generosity of a donor, Mr. James Wiley, Texas A&M began adding CD-ROM workstations for a number of databases. Currently there are twenty-eight databases on CD-ROM, being run on twenty-five stations. These are available on a "first come, first served" basis, unless someone requests a particular database currently in use. In that instance, the individual currently using the system is limited to 30 minutes.[2]

Administering an Enduser Program

When the BRS After Dark program began, librarians worked in the area and monitored the searches, logging on and off the systems, keeping records and advising patrons on searches. It quickly became apparent that patrons were not utilizing the technology to their best advantage. While the systems were billed as user friendly, many patrons did not fully understand the strategies of searching, including the use of boolean operators and appropriate keywords. While they might achieve a large number of hits, and indeed were often impressed with that high number of hits, they failed to realize that the incidence of such high numbers meant that they had not qualified their search structures to retrieve truly pertinent citations. The staff found that patrons were impressed by the technology itself, entranced with the speed of retrieval, but failed to realize that the true value of the system went beyond speed. They were unaware of the fact that it allowed them to refine their searches to retrieve the best citations on a subject. Indeed, the online systems allowed them to narrow their searches far better than they could in a paper search.

The Evans Library therefore began to develop ideas regarding training endusers. As the number of available databases and terminals increased, it became apparent that whoever was monitoring the search area simply could not train each individual. Time alone was an inhibiting factor and the constraints of staffing did not allow placing additional individuals in the searching area.

Developing an Instructional Program for Endusers

The instructional program began with the development a brief slide tape that could be mounted on an individualized viewing machine and the requirement that all first time users needed to watch this fifteen minute program before being allowed online. The tape covered basics such as what an online database included, how to formulate searches and the use of boolean operators. Examples were given and users were urged to develop keywords and a simplified strategy before reporting to the area for their search.

With the increasing use of this program, the Library realized that they had to have additional means of teaching endusers how to search. It was becoming unrealistic to have one slide/tape show available for viewing. Sheer numbers prohibited many users having a chance to view it prior to their search. Several librarians therefore explored alternative instructional methods, such as a CAI program and a users manual. These methods were tested, evaluating the searches of first time users and comparing the three methods employed. The results of this study proved that the users manual was the most effective method.[3] In addition, it could be easily mass produced at a minimal cost. A large number of users could be reached at any given time without a great deal of expense.

All first time users were required to read the manual prior to their search. They were instructed to do this at the time of their appointment and warned that it took approximately 40 minutes to read the manual and they should plan for this prior to appearing for their search. In addition, a profiling sheet was developed which they were instructed to have filled out when they came to the searching area. This is the current situation and continues to work efficiently. There is now a clerk who is hired to monitor the searching area and she is assisted by student workers. Appointments are taken through the reference. Reference librarians are always available to provide assistance and/or advice, while the BRS Clerk also goes over the searching profile prior to logging the enduser online.

Therefore, when Texas A&M began adding CD-ROM database to the enduser program, a system was already in place that could serve as a model for training endusers in the application of this new technology.

The Impact of CD-ROM Searching

As the number of available CD-ROM workstations increased, Evans Library began purchasing a number of different vendor products, which utilized different search strategies, and it was apparent that we could not produce a single manual that would cover all necessities for CD-ROM searching. Accordingly, as new products came in, they were assigned to different librarians, giving them a responsibility for a new system in their area of expertise. In other words, a science reference librarian would be given the responsibility to learn about the Life Sciences database and a social sciences librarian would do the same with PsycLit. Each librarian would then learn all the modifications of searching on their databases and be responsible for teaching others about it. In addition, one of their prime responsibilities was to prepare a searching guide for that database. These were not envisioned as a lengthy manual, but were developed as quick reference guides that could be placed next to the workstation for consultation when needed by the patron. In addition, someone was stationed in the workstation area during all hours of staffing. In order to avoid continued drain on available staff, it was decided to use student workers in this area, and extra work study students were hired.

For many years, student workers had been used as backup on our reference desk, and assigned reference desk duties during the evenings and weekends. They were used to working with the patrons. They were now trained to work in the CD-ROM area, and taught how to monitor the equipment and help the patrons with their searches. A reference librarian was always available for consultation if needed.[4]

This type of staffing has worked well. The majority of patrons like to have someone nearby to question when needed, and it appears that the majority of the student workers like this part of their work assignment and quickly develop a sense of searching expertise that is beneficial to patrons and staff alike. The drawbacks, however, remain. They are centered around time and the fact that student workers are not professionals. They can generally answer search questions and assist the patrons, but they cannot deal with detailed searching problems and they are not good at recommending alternative sources when CD-ROM databases do not supply sufficient information or are not applicable for the patron's needs. They do not have the time to teach in-depth searching strategy to individuals and must divide their attention among a variety of products and individuals.

These online and ondisk databases are extremely popular. Recent statistics in the CD-ROM area alone show that over 100 users per day are taking advantage of these products. Reference librarians tend to refer patrons to these indexes rather than demonstrate the use of corresponding paper indexes. Few professionals and support staff guide patrons to such traditional tools as Psychological Abstracts, Bibliography of Agriculture, or Dissertation Abstracts, when they know that the patron can achieve his needs more rapidly by doing an ondisk or online search. The patrons help advertise these services and many of them now approach the Reference Desk asking about such searches and have been known to express disappointment when a database is not available for their particular discipline or research needs.

Training CD-ROM Endusers

Such increased use of these services has meant that library staff needed to develop a variety of teaching methods to train endusers for CD-ROM searching. The components of poor searches that were noted several years ago with the introduction of enduser searching for our online systems, are still present with the availability of ondisk searches. They are multiplied as access to this type of service has increased.

Accordingly, the Evans Library realized the need to teach groups of endusers as an enhancement to its one-to-one instruction being conducted in the workstation area. It was obvious that it would not be possible to develop a single manual that would cover all aspects of CD-ROM searching. Librarians were not dealing with one or two systems, as they had been with the BRS After Dark program. They therefore began to develop instructional programs that could be carried into the classroom setting or used in the group instruction rooms of the library. In conjunction with a Public Relations campaign to advertise the availability of these new services, they also offered demonstrations that would enable patrons to better use these systems.

Equipment for Group Instruction

In order to perform these demonstrations, the library began examining equipment that would enable them to perform ondisk demonstrations using a large screen projector which would transmit the image from a monitor to a screen. In the fall of 1987, they purchased a Limelight projection system and began using it with a Compaq I computer. The Limelight was then one of the few large screen projectors on the market and staff were pleased to have it. It was, however, bulky to use and difficult to transport. It also gave a monochromatic image with poor resolution. It did, however, enable librarians to perform demonstrations for groups and teach some of the fundamentals of searching with the possibility of hands-on experience prior to a patron actually performing their own search.

In the following year, a Datashow from Kodak was purchased which allowed much better resolution, was easy to transport and fit on top of an overhead projector to allow onscreen projection from a computer monitor. This continued to be used in conjunction with Compaqs I and II.

The continuing demand for online and ondisk teaching demonstrations has since required purchase of additional equipment, a MagnaByte projector from Telex, which is similar to the Datashow but allows color projection if one is demonstrating a color database. It also fits on top of an overhead projector and is easily transported for offsite demonstrations. The Library has also ordered another liquid crystal display pad from Dukane which will project 16 colors.

Methodology for Group Instruction

These equipment purchases have meant that reference librarians are able to go into the classroom or any group situation and teach the refinements of database searching, whether that is related to online or ondisk databases. They attempt to fit teaching methods to the needs of the audience. Subject searches will therefore depend upon the discipline and they will attempt to develop search strategies based upon topics that would interest the particular audience. The librarians, however, attempt to cover certain basic aspects of database searching, whatever the subject discipline being covered. They explain what a database is and attempt to relate it to the printed index with which many of the audience will be familiar. They then explain how the computer is searching this database, emphasizing that it can only do what it is commanded. Attempts are then made to detail the basics of boolean logic, noting the different results achieved by using different boolean operators in a search. Also covered are the use of keywords, truncation and how to limit by such items as language and date of publication. Whenever possible, members of the group are allowed to have some hands-on experience and to construct a search around their interests. In each instance, handouts are furnished that explain the basics of boolean searching and profiling sheets are passed out that let endusers design a search strategy. These types of group demonstrations are an invaluable aid in preparing endusers for individual searches. When they appear for either an online or an ondisk search, they have some background that enriches whatever assistance they may receive from individualized instruction in the searching area. The two methods complement each other and work in tandem to enable endusers to use these systems to their best advantage.

In addition, staff members also developed a canned program using ShowPartner presentation software. This program enabled training presentations to be done where online or laserdisk demonstrations were not feasible.[5]

THE PROBLEM OF REMOTE USERS

The issue of remote users presents still additional problems to librarians. There exists an audience who may be searching library databases without entering the library or having access to a librarian. The most common aspect of this is usually remote access to a library's online catalog. There may also be users who are accessing the same databases that are searched at the library, but experience shows that the majority of these will have had to arrange their own passwords and are experienced in searching the particular database that is relevant to their field. They rarely have to call upon the expertise of the librarian and will be training themselves from manuals supplied by a vendor. The online catalog, however, is often the most highly used database by a campus and one over whose development librarians will have had some control.

The Sterling C. Evans Library inaugurated a new online catalog in the autumn of 1988. A previous online system allowed searching by author, title, and call number and was run off an in-house mainframe. Remote users employed a modem and simply dialed into the mainframe through a limited number of ports. Author/title searching required little explanation and we rarely had questions regarding assistance. With the installation of NOTIS, however, users had the option of title, author, subject and keyword searching, the latter employing boolean operators and BRS protocols. Remote users would now be able to perform searches similar to those being done on in-house databases and experience had taught a need to particularly train them in regard to the use of keyword searching.

In addition, the new online catalog would be run off the mainframe at the campus Computer Services Center, readily available through a campus network. The Library was also aware that the era of the dumb terminal was over and that people throughout the campus, or off campus, would be using a variety of communications packages to communicate with the mainframe.

Instructional Materials for Remote Users

The initial problem was to develop guides that would teach remote users the methods of logging into and off the system. Staff began by approaching the Computer Services Center and learning what were the most common communications packages on the campus. Five major ones in use were identified and instructions written for each of them. These were then combined in a manual for remote users, which included a basic introduction for microcomputer access to the online catalog and then referred the user to a different section depending upon what communications package he/she might use.

At the same time, a searching guide for the online catalog was developed that examined the different types of searches available in NOTIS and gave examples. A large portion of this dealt with keyword searches and the use of boolean operators, truncation, and possible refinements of search strategy. We also paid attention to the design of our screens, with a particular concern for the remote user. Attempts were made to make them be as self-explanatory as possible, and special concern was given to the help screens for each of the different types of searches.

Having developed these aids and screen modifications, a campus-wide mailout of NOTIS promotion material was made. In the handout, faculty members were offered the option of an individual instruction in the Reference office, a classroom or group demonstration and details were given about the availability of handouts for remote users. The brochure had a tear off sheet whereby the faculty member could check what items were of interest to them and return it to the library. In response, the Library mailed them the required information and contacted those who were interested in a demonstration or individual instruction.

Group Training for Remote Users

It was fortunate that previously purchased equipment used in group demonstrations for online and ondisk searching was in place to be employed in training remote users. Staff have seen an increasing demand for NOTIS demonstrations during the past year, to classes, seminars and faculty/staff groups. They have approached these in the same manner as other training demonstrations, attempting to cover the basics of searching. In addition, however, they have shown the groups how to access the catalog from a remote site, dialing into the system using a modem and a software communications package. Using a COMPAQ I or COMPAQ II, an overhead projector and one of the large screen projection systems, the audience was able to watch staff access the catalog in the same manner that they would as remote users. This was followed with a demonstration on the different types of searches available in NOTIS, paying particular attention to keyword and employing the same teaching methods that were used in online and ondisk demonstrations.

There continue to exist problems with remote users, the primary one being that many of those accessing the card catalog never contact the library for instructions or handouts. They simply see the availability of NOTIS on the campus system and attempt to log in. The staff began getting a large number of telephone calls from these types of remote users, who were attempting to access and search the catalog with no instruction.

In an attempt to reach some solution, all staff members were required to learn how to access the catalog using each of the different communications packages that were detailed in the remote users manual. They also learned all the refinements of searching the catalog and received practicums over remote access and possible search questions. The result has been that whenever a remote user calls into the library, someone will be available who can answer his questions and help him over the telephone. In each instance, the staff ask for the person's name and address and inform him that the Library will be happy to send written instructions and a searching guide.

CONCLUSION

In conclusion, training endusers and remote users requires flexibility. No one training plan appears to be the final answer. If you rely upon a one-to-one situation based upon your workstation area, you will find that there simply is not enough time to teach the refinements of database searching. Group sessions allow more time, enable an instructor to reach a larger audience and permit some hands-on experience prior to a patron actually performing a search. They do, however, require special projection equipment and a compatible, portable computer in order to be effective. In addition, you must have clear, concise written materials to support whatever oral presentation/teaching method you are using.

In the case of remote users, written handouts become all important, since librarians may never come into contact with these users. It is highly advisable to have all staff fully trained to answer telephone questions for remote users.

The advent of new technologies has changed the teaching role of librarians, and it is vital that we develop the means to train our patrons to fully utilize these new services. We must be adaptable to the situation and realize that we are still teaching, still guiding our users to their information needs. Training has become more important than ever.

REFERENCES

1. Jaros, Joe with Vicki Anders and Geraldine Hutchins, "Subsidized End-User Searching in an Academic Library." *Proceedings of the Seventh National Online Meeting, New York, May 6-8, 1986.* Medford, New Jersey: Learned Information, pp. 223-229.

2. Jackson, Kathy M. with Evelyn M. King and Jean Kellough, "How to Organize an Extensive Laserdisk Installation: The Texas A&M Experience." *Online* 12(2), March 1988, pp. 51-60.

3. Hutchins, Geraldine with Joe Jaros and Vicki Anders, "End-User Perceptions of Teaching Methods." *Proceedings of the Eighth National Online Meeting May 5-7, 1987*. Medford, New Jersey: Learned Information, pp. 183-190.

4. Tucker, Sandra L. with Vicki Anders, Katharine E. Clark, and William R. Kinyon, "How to Manage an Extensive Laserdisk Installation: The Texas A&M Experience." *Online* 12(3), May 1988, pp. 34-46.

5. Charles, Susan K. with Keith A. Waddle, and Jacqueline B. Hambric, "Using Presentation Software to Train Laserdisk Database Users." *Laserdisk Professional*, 1(4), November 1988, pp. 91-95.

Student Staff Training in the Smaller Library

Ruth Ann Edwards

SUMMARY. Students are increasingly filling crucial roles in the smaller undergraduate college library, a convenient on-campus setting for work-study assignments. The one-on-one training pattern predominates and is effective at Randolph-Macon Woman's College, an institution where education in the singular is stressed. The various departments detail modes of interaction between supervisor/student staff member. Shortcomings as well as strengths are acknowledged.

In the not too distant past, only professionally trained librarians were entrusted with many aspects of technical and public service work in the academic library. Now, in the experience of this small and increasingly automated academic library, students are filling a crucial role in many of the operations.

Donald G. Frank, in his discussion of the student assistants in the academic library, stresses the value of hiring based upon criteria that include attitude, employment experience, academic credentials, graduation date, hours available for work and potential communication skills.[1] Would that such luxury were always possible.

In the undergraduate women's college setting, those students that are receiving financial aid form the bulk of the labor pool as every effort is made by the college to fit student need to campus job. In general, the students' motivation for fulfilling the demands of

---

Ruth Ann Edwards is Director of the Library at Randolph-Macon Woman's College in Lynchburg, VA.

The author acknowledges the assistance of staff members, Brenda Bateman, Catalog Librarian; Jean H. Wilson, Assistant Cataloger; Jan P. Johnson, Collection Development Librarian and Patricia M. DeMars, Reference Librarian.

© 1990 by The Haworth Press, Inc. All rights reserved.

work-study schedule with a library position is a positive factor, but not always is the library best served in this context.

Ultimately, the ability to turn the raw recruit into a valued co-worker rests with staff supervisors as they guide students to achieve personal growth in service to library goals.

THE ADVANTAGE OF ONE-ON-ONE; THE INFORMAL

The major difference between student assistant training in a small library setting and a large one is the extent of formal structure necessary to communicate. In large departments where there are many students to be trained, it is more practical to use the classroom approach and teach many at one time. This usually requires written instructions or procedures to which the students may refer.

When meeting with many students at once, one can make certain that all receive the same information. Instruction can include policies, expectations and responsibilities in an organized and impartial manner so that each student receives the same message, making misunderstandings unlikely. Role playing is also effective in this type of training. Students can take on the role of patron and subsequently, librarian for a better understanding of how to deal with encounters from both sides of the desk.

Even in the smaller college environment, orientation, explanation and group teaching are rarely possible. However, in library departments with a few student assistants, librarians can interact on the personal, one-on-one level. Teaching becomes "showing" whereby the staff member leads the student through all steps of a procedure or task, and instructions are conveyed verbally.

The one-on-one informal approach is effective because it is "task-intensive." The student learns a task by actually doing it with another. In most functions within the academic setting, we find that students learn well from other students, and a well trained student assistant can become an asset in training others.

At Randolph-Macon *Woman*'s College, in keeping with our emphasis on education in the singular, it has been effective to maintain the individual approach to strengthen the positive working relationship and rapport between student and supervisor.

Procedures in the Cataloging Department

Student applicants are interviewed individually by the supervising librarian. The various tasks done by students are outlined and it is pointed out honestly that some of them are repetitive and "dull." Candidates are asked if they are able to adapt to work requiring great attention to detail. If not, they seek assignment elsewhere.

When a new student reports for work, the supervising librarian shows her around the department and gives her a brief outline of department goals, so that she will have a rationale for the jobs she is assigned. It is stressed that although it is possible to be more flexible about work hours in cataloging than in circulation, it is still necessary for the student to give notice if unable to report so that her tasks may be reassigned.

Also, in order to avoid rampant absenteeism, a form has been devised in which students agree to work half-time during exam week. Future employment in the library is contingent upon fulfilling this requirement. Students may work exam week hours all in one day, at night or on weekends during exam week.

Brief daily work slips are written for each student as assurance that the tasks will be given the necessary priority whether or not the supervising librarian is at hand.

The librarian supervisor usually gets the student started on each new job to ensure a thorough understanding of the project. With the exception of the simplest routines, experience has shown it is unwise to relegate this phase of teaching to the peer teacher.

In the past, many hours have been spent teaching catalog filing. (We hope that in another year this function will be obsolete!) To a small group of 3 or 4 students, general catalog filing is explained. Over the years, the cataloger has kept a list of problems that seem to recur for student filers, and these are explained. In actual filing, each student records the area in which she files, i.e., Sarah—drawers 518-712. Schedules are arranged so that no one files more than one hour at a time. As she files, each filing is flagged and the card dropped. As the filing is revised by the cataloging staff, a slip with corrections is made for each filer. For the first few months, each error is written up as follows: drawer 520—new edition files in front; drawer 523—alphabet!; drawer 540—note sub-head of time period, etc. Students are given the corrections and asked to go correct them, reflagging. The corrections are rechecked in the next revision. Although these steps are cumbersome, they appear to achieve the end result of relatively accurate student filers. Several students have even admitted it as a plus for them academically: "Now I can find anything in the catalog!"

It has been the feeling of this department that acquiring good work habits is a part of the whole learning process. Many times college supervisors are contacted for job recommendations for students after graduation. In other words, the library work experience is a real job.

As an expression of appreciation, students are often remembered with some token at holiday times. Where but in the smaller setting are such personal touches applied?

Working with student assistants can be trying at times; it also has its rewards as one observes growth and maturity over four years. Occasional visits or letters from former student staff members make us realize that working in the library has been a vital part of their college experience.

Acquisitions

Acquisition procedures that exist in written form are given to the students to read. Procedures that can only be explained verbally are done so when each situation arises.

The acquisitions librarian supervises but other students and library clerical staff do the actual one-on-one training. Fortuitously, one large room for technical processing provides the opportunity to hear and see questionable shortcuts or non-standard methods. Direct observation allows the supervisor to evaluate the quality of students' work as well as their comprehension of procedures.

Students rely on staff to solve unusual problems but the troubleshooting process which the staff member employs is communicated back to the student for future use. As students understand the complete work flow, they are able to recognize and solve more possible problems on their own. One-on-one training is most valuable in acquisitions.

Circulation

After the introductory session, experienced students train others in the various procedures in the circulation department. This is a situation where new students gain confidence from working with a peer teacher, where fears are minimized and a comfortable learning situation is created.

After new students are familiar with the basic tasks, the circulation supervisor revises; when enough time has elapsed for a new student to be conversant with all the tasks for which she is responsible, she is given a checklist. If the trainee indicates a lack of knowledge for any given task on the list, the supervisor takes time to again demonstrate the procedure and gives examples to reinforce.

In general, the student assistants in the circulation area soon develop pride in their essential, center stage position, backed up by a supervisor who makes it abundantly clear that, if needed, she is no farther than a phone call away. On campus, back-up and support are provided by Security in the event of any serious emergency.

Reference

Students from the pool are screened for employment on the following criteria: their interest, suitable schedule, and year (freshmen are preferred for the sake of continuity).

Tasks for student assistants are assigned on an individual basis with each student having different responsibilities or special projects. Training is done on a one-to-one basis. A few jobs typically assigned to students are: setting up displays, serving as archives or research assistant, operating the fax, shelving, telephone answering, desk duty.

Student training consists of three components. The first component is orientation. All students begin with a lesson on the library's classification system and are shown the location of the reference materials; introductions are made to staff and other students; schedule and work patterns are established; guidelines for behavior are set.

The second training component is an explanation of policies, procedures and duties. The "why's" as well as the "how's" are included in this phase of training. Because Reference is a service department, it is important that all members of Reference give pleasant and efficient service. Obviously, inadequate training will result in poor service. A training environment in which positive attitudes develop is essential.

Follow-up is the last component of training. All students are reviewed for competency, given feedback and encouragement. Much is done to make the student feel confident and secure. Levels of responsibility are increased as competency increases.

At some point during the year, students are asked to evaluate their training so that we as supervisors are given feedback and an opportunity to improve as well.

PITFALLS AND HAZARDS OF THE INFORMAL MODE

There is always the risk of the system becoming too casual. The staff manual may not always be assigned reading for newcomers. Introductions of each new student may not include the entire staff; some essential may be overlooked, i.e., emergency procedures not given in a timely fashion nor made clear. Omissions can occur on the assumption that someone else has taken care of the instructions. Not enough effort is spent relating the specific to the whole. Continuity may be lost. Enough satisfactory supervisor/student overlap may not occur because of a daily schedule that must cover 16 hours plus a seven day week. Students may of necessity be scheduled on their own before they have mastered the range of essential procedures. We risk the syndrome of a Jill of all trades, mistress of none.

VALUES AND STRENGTHS OF STUDENT STAFF PARTICIPATION IN THE SMALLER LIBRARY

For many students, working in the Lipscomb Library may be their first employment experience. Opportunities can be seized or ignored according to the personality of the student. Opportunities exist in the library to build positive working relationships between supervisors and co-workers, to develop initiative and leadership and to use the experience as a springboard to meet and accept responsibilities that will be met in the work-a-day life after college.

The library on the other hand, depends upon student assistants as an integral element of the staff. As we teach, supervise and train a segment of the student body each year, we keep in touch with the current youth culture as we clarify our own command of changes in library practice. We are bonded in a model symbiosis.

NOTE

1. Donald G. Frank, "Management of Student Assistants in a Public Services Setting of an Academic Library," *RQ*, 24:51 (Fall 1984).